The secret of
happy
children

HarperCollins*Publishers*

First published in Australia in 1984 by Bay Books
Revised edition 1988, reprinted in 1992
Revised edition 1993, reprinted in 1993, 1994
Angus & Robertson edition 1995
Reprinted in 1996, 1997
This HarperCollins edition 1998
by HarperCollins*Publishers* Pty Limited
ACN 009 913 517
A member of the HarperCollins*Publishers* (Australia) Pty Limited Group
http://www.harpercollins.com.au

HarperCollins*Publishers*
25 Ryde Road, Pymble, Sydney, NSW 2073, Australia
31 View Road, Glenfield, Auckland 10, New Zealand
77–85 Fulham Palace Road, London W6 8JB, United Kingdom
Hazelton Lanes, 55 Avenue Road, Suite 2900, Toronto, Ontario M5R 3L2
and 1995 Markham Road, Scarborough, Ontario M1B 5M8, Canada
10 East 53rd Street, New York NY 10032, USA

National Library of Australia Cataloguing-in-Publication data:

Biddulph, Steve.
The secret of happy children.
Rev. ed.
ISBN 0 7322 5842 1.
1. Child rearing. 2 Parenting. 3. Parent and child.
4. Child psychology. I. Title
649.1

Cartoons by Allan Stomann
Illustrations by Paul Stanish
Cover design: Miller Hare
Cover photo: Raph and Lucy Giarrupto, courtesy Alison Bennett
Printed in Australia by Griffin Press Pty Ltd, Adelaide on 65gsm Bulky Paperback

9 8 7 6 5 4 3 2 1   98 99 00 01

The secret of
happy
children

Steve Biddulph

Cartoons by Allan Stomann

HarperCollins*Publishers*

Thanks to all in the Transactional Analysis community from the early seventies onwards, especially Colin McKenzie, Pat McKenzie, the Maslens, the Mellors, and Jean Grigor. These people both saved my life, and sent me on this wonderful road. To my parents for a good beginning. To my incomparable partner Shaaron Biddulph. To Robin Freeman, Phillipa Sandall, Rex Finch and present and past editors at HarperCollins. And to all parents everywhere, for struggling on and still remembering how to laugh.

Contents

The story behind this book.

When I first wrote *The Secret of Happy Children*, I never dreamed that it would take off in quite the way it has. Fourteen years after first firing up the typewriter, it has been read by over a million people, in fourteen languages.

When I wrote *The Secret* I was just a beginning Family Therapist, with a heartfelt wish to make it easier for fathers and mothers to get along well with their kids, and for kids to live without the put-downs and fears that our generation often felt.

The first edition announced on the opening page that I had no children, only wombats (and that these were quite badly behaved!). I mentioned this because it was true, and because I wanted my readers to take everything I said with a pinch of salt – to trust their own judgement. I still believe this – experts are a hazard to your family! If you listen to your own heart it will always tell you what is the best way to raise your children. Books, experts, friends, help you only if they take you closer to your own good sense.

I do have kids of my own now, and the wombats have all grown up! But my feelings haven't changed. I still get a melting feeling in my chest when I see a young mother with a new baby, or a young father playing with his kids. I'm more impressed by young parents and their efforts than by any sports hero, rock star, or business tycoon!

Anyhow, I'm proud to be launching this new reprint. Many hundreds of parents have told me that they found the ideas in this book powerful and helpful. Much that they have taught me has been incorporated to make the book even better.

Hope you like it.

Steve Biddulph

Foreword

Why are so many adults unhappy?

Think of all the people you know who have problems – who lack confidence, cannot make a decision, can't relax, or can't make friends with other people. Think of those who are aggressive, putting people down and ignoring the needs of those around them. Add to the above all those just holding on until the next drink or the next tranquilliser.

In one of the richest, most peaceful countries in the world, unhappiness is epidemic. One adult in every five will at some time need psychiatric care, one marriage in three ends in divorce, one adult in four needs medication to relax. It's a great life!

Unemployment and difficult economic times don't help, but unhappiness is present in all income groups – rich, poor and in-between. It's a problem, in fact, that no amount of money seems to solve.

On the plus side, we are often struck by some people's constant cheerfulness and optimism. Why is it that, in some individuals, the human spirit blossoms in spite of apparent hardship?

The simple fact is many people have unhappiness programmed into them. They have been unwittingly taught as children to be unhappy, and are now living out the script. Through reading this book you may discover that, by accident, you are hypnotising your children into disliking themselves, and causing them to have problems which may last a lifetime.

But this need not be so. You can program your children to be optimistic, loving, capable and happy. To have a good chance of a long, successful life. So let's begin ...

1

Seeds in the mind

**You hypnotise your children
every single day. You may as well
do it properly!**

It's 9 o'clock at night and I'm sitting in my office with a tearful fifteen-year-old girl. She wears make-up and is dressed in fashionable, older-than-her-years clothes, but the effect is only to make her look more helpless and childlike. We are talking about the fact that she is pregnant and what can be done about it.

This is familiar ground for me, and for anyone who works with teenagers. It doesn't mean, though, that it can be hurried. What matters is that, for the young woman sitting in front of me, this is the worst day of her life and she needs all the support, time and clarity, that I can muster. Above all she must make her own right decision.

I ask about her parents' likely reaction – when they find out. She almost spits out the answer.

> 'Oh, they'll say they told me so. They always said I'd never amount to nuthin'!'

Later, as I drive home, that one sentence stays in my mind. 'They always said I'd never amount to nothing.' I've often heard parents talk to kids like that.

> 'You're hopeless.'
> 'God, you're a nuisance.'
> 'You'll be sorry, just you see.'
> 'You're as bad as your Uncle Merv' (who's in jail).
> 'You're just like your Auntie Eve' (who's fond of a drink).
> 'You're crazy, do you hear?'

This is the kind of programming that many youngsters grow up with; it is passed on unthinkingly by stressed-out parents and continues as a kind of family curse down the generations. It's called a *self-fulfilling prophecy* because saying it often enough makes it come true. Children, with their brilliant, perceptive ways, will usually live up to our expectations!

These are extreme examples, which we'd all recognise at once as destructive. Most negative programming, however, is much more subtle. Observe children playing in a vacant block, climbing trees. 'You'll fall! Watch out! You'll slip!' cries the voice of their anxious mother from over the fence.

The half drunk father ends a half-hearted argument with his wife, who goes off in a 'huff' to buy some cigarettes. 'There y'are son, never trust a woman. They'll just use y'up.' The seven-year-old looks up solemnly and nods. Yes, Dad.

And, in a million living rooms and kitchens:

'God, you're lazy'
'You're so selfish'
'You silly idiot, stop that'
'Dumb'
'Give it to me, stupid'
'Don't be such a pest.'

This kind of talk doesn't just make a child feel bad momentarily. Put-downs also have a hypnotic effect and act unconsciously, like seeds in the mind, seeds which will grow and shape the child's self-image, eventually becoming part of their personality.

How do we hypnotise our children?

Hypnosis and suggestion have long been a source of fascination to people. They seem slightly mystical and unreal and yet are well accepted scientifically. Most people have witnessed them, perhaps as part of a stage show, or for getting help to stop smoking, or on a relaxation tape.

We are familiar with the key elements of hypnosis: the use of some device to distract the mind ('Vatch ze vatch'), the commanding tone ('You are feeling sleepy!'), and the rhythmic, repetitious tone of the hypnotist's speech ('Hey! Wake up!'). We also know about post-hypnotic suggestion, the ability to implant a command which the unsuspecting person later carries out, often to his or her dismay, at a given signal. It all makes for good theatre, but also for excellent therapy in the hands of a qualified practitioner.

What most people don't realise, though, is that *hypnosis is an everyday event*. Whenever we use certain patterns of speech, we reach into the unconscious minds of our children and program them, even though we have no such intention.

The old concept – that hypnosis required an altered state of mind, or trance, has been abandoned. This was only one form of unconscious learning. The rather frightening truth is that the human mind can be

programmed in normal waking life beneath the awareness of the person involved. Already in the US, many sales and advertising people as well as lawyers are being trained in the use of hypnotic methods embedded in normal business conversation – a scary concept. Fortunately hypnosis can be countered if the subject becomes aware of the process. Accidental hypnosis, though, is part of everyday life. Parents – without realising it – implant messages in their child's mind, and these messages, unless strongly contradicted, will echo on for a lifetime.

HYPNOTISED WITHOUT KNOWING IT

The late Dr Milton Erikson was recognised as the world's foremost hypnotist. He was once called upon to treat a man who suffered extreme pain from cancer, was refusing to have hypnosis and was not being helped by painkillers. Erikson simply stopped by his private ward and talked about the man's hobby of growing tomatoes.

A careful listener could have detected the unusual rhythm in Erikson's speech and, the stressing of odd phrases, like 'deep down' (in the soil), growing 'good and strong', 'easy' (to pick), 'warm and loose' (in the glasshouse). Also, the observer could have noted that Erikson's face and posture changed very slightly as he spoke those key phrases. The man in question simply thought that it was a pleasant exchange. Until he died, however, five days later, as doctors knew he must, the man felt no further pain.

'You' messages

A child's mind is full of questions. Perhaps the greatest of these are the questions, 'Who am I?', 'What kind of person am I?', 'Where do I fit in?'. These are the questions of self-definition, or identity, upon which we base our lives as adults, and from which we make all our key decisions. A child's mind is remarkably affected by statements which begin with the words, 'You are'.

Whether the message is 'You are so lazy' or 'You're a great kid', these statements from the important 'big' people will go deeply and firmly into the child's unconsciousness. I have heard so many adults, overcome by a life crisis, recalling what they were told as a child: 'I'm so useless, I know I am'.

Imagine how differently your child's life will turn out if they have the following beliefs about themselves …

- I am a good person.
- I can get on well with most people.
- I can usually figure things out.
- I have a good brain.
- I'm really creative.
- My body is healthy and strong.
- I like the way I look
… and so on!

Psychologists (who love to complicate things) call these statements 'attributions'. These attributions crop up again and again in adult life.

'Why don't you apply for that promotion?'
'No, I'm not good enough.'
'But he's just like your last husband. Why did you marry him?'
'I'm just stupid, I guess.'
'Why do you let them push you around like that?'
'That's the story of my life.'

These words – 'not good enough', 'just stupid' – did not come out of the blue. They are recorded in people's brains because they were said to them at an age when they were unable to question their truthfulness. 'But surely,' I can hear you saying, 'children must disagree with the "you" messages they are given?'.

Certainly children think about the things that are said to them, checking for accuracy. But they may have no comparisons. At times we are all lazy, selfish, untidy, stupid, forgetful, mischievous, and so on. The fire-and-brimstone preacher in the old-time church was on a sure thing when he thundered out, 'You have sinned!' – everyone had!

'Adults know everything; they can even read your mind.' Such are the thoughts of a child. So when a child is told 'You're clumsy', he or she becomes nervous, and clumsy. The child told 'You're a pest' feels the rejection, becomes desperate for reassurance and so does pester. The child told 'You're an idiot' may violently disagree on the outside, but inside can only sadly agree. You're the adult, so you must be right.

'You' messages work at *both* the conscious and unconscious levels. In my clinical work I've often asked children to describe themselves, and they will say things like 'I'm a bad kid', 'I'm a nuisance.'

Others, though, will show evidence of confusion — 'Mum and Dad say they love me, but I don't think they do'. Consciously they hear the words, but unconsciously they hear/see/smell a different feeling behind the words.

It's all in the way we say it. We can choose to say to children, 'I'm angry with you and I want you to tidy up your toys NOW!' and have no fears about lasting effects. If we say, 'You lazy little brat, why don't you ever do what you're told?' and repeat this kind of message whenever conflict occurs, then the result will come as no surprise.

Don't pretend to be happy or loving when you aren't feeling that way — it's confusing and can make children become evasive and in time quite disturbed. We can be honest about our feelings, without putting children down. They can handle 'I'm really tired today', or 'Right now I'm too angry'. . . especially if this matches what their senses are telling them. It helps them realise that you are human too, which has got to be a good thing.

At a large parents' meeting I once addressed, I asked if people would call out the 'you' messages they remembered hearing as children. I wrote them on a whiteboard and this is what we came up with:

You're lazy clumsy stupid
a nuisance just a girl
too young to understand
selfish dumb
a pest dirty
thoughtless inconsiderate
always late greedy
bad-tempered brainless noisy
gutless a worry crazy
mental making your mother sick
ugly plain immature
just like your father
...and on it went.

The examples came in little rushes at first, as people's memories were triggered, but by the end the whiteboard was covered and the room was almost in a state of riot. The sense of relief and release was very evident in the large hall as people spoke aloud the words that had hurt them so long ago.

Very few people felt their parents had been deliberately destructive or malicious — it was simply that this was the way children were corrected. 'Tell them they're bad and that makes them good!' Those were the Dark Ages of child-rearing: we're just beginning to escape.

YOUR MIND REMEMBERS EVERYTHING THAT EVER HAPPENED TO YOU

In the 1950s people with epilepsy had a bad time because the medications we now use had not been developed. A man called Penfield found that an operation could be used to help the more severe cases. By making small cuts on the surface of a person's brain, he could sometimes reduce or even halt the 'electrical storms' which cause epileptic seizures.

The interesting part — I hope you're sitting down as you read this — is that patients were required, for safety reasons, to be conscious, and the operation was done under only a local anaesthetic. The surgeon removed a small piece of skull, made the cuts and then put back the piece and sewed up the skin. It makes me shudder, too, but it was better than the disease!

During the operation, the patients experienced something very surprising. As the doctor, using a fine probe, delicately touched the surface of the brain, the patient would suddenly have vivid recollections — watching *Gone with the Wind* years earlier, complete with the smell of cheap perfume in the cinema and the beehive hairstyle of the person in front! When the doctor moved the probe to another spot, the person would see before him his fourth birthday even though he was wide awake and sitting in the operating chair. It was the same with every patient, though of course the memories were different.

Subsequent research backed up this remarkable discovery: that everything — every sight, sound, and spoken word — is stored forever in our brain, along with the emotions we felt at the time. It is often difficult to remember but nonetheless it is there, having its effect. On the wrinkled surface of our brain our life is recorded in its entirety!

Unconscious hearing is another phenomenon that you've almost certainly experienced. You've been at a party or a meeting, listening to someone near you. The room is buzzing with people talking and perhaps music, too. Suddenly, from a conversation clear across the room, you hear someone say your name, or the name of a friend, or something that concerns you. 'Aaargh!' you think, 'what are they saying about me?'.

How does this happen? We have discovered from research that there are two parts to your hearing: firstly, what your ears actually pick up; and secondly, what you pay conscious attention to.

Although you are unaware of it, your brilliant hearing system is filtering every conversation within range in the room and, if a key word or phrase occurs, the switchboard department in your brain 'puts it through' to conscious attention. You certainly couldn't listen to all that was being said at one time but, nonetheless, a primitive filter is scanning it for important messages. We know this from many experiments and also from the fact that under hypnosis people can recall things that they *didn't consciously notice at the time*!

The following situation has been reported in many parts of the world.

Late one night a semi-trailer runs out of control, careers downhill and smashes through the front wall of a house. When rescuers enter the house they are amazed to find a young mother sleeping heavily, undisturbed by the crash. As they stand there, not knowing what to do, a baby begins to cry in the back room. The mother instantly awakes. 'Wha ... what's going on?'

The filter in her hearing system works on as she sleeps but is checking for only one thing – the baby – and only this sound is 'put through' to her awareness.

How does all of the above relate to children? Think of all the things that are said about children when they are supposedly not listening. Then remember their acute listening powers (a lolly wrapper at 50 metres!). We may well include the time when they are asleep for there is clear evidence that sounds and speech are taken in even as a person dreams and sleeps.

Also, there is that obvious time when a child has not yet learned (or decided to let you know) that it can speak. A toddler, for months before it speaks much, can follow much of what is intended, if not every word.

I am often amazed by parents, who have been fighting bitterly for years or are desperately unhappy for some reason, telling me, 'Of course, the kids know nothing about it'. Children, in fact, know almost everything about everything. They may oblige you by keeping it to themselves or only show it indirectly by bedwetting or trying to murder their siblings, but they know. So, if you talk about your children, be sure you are saying what you really want to say. This, too, is a direct channel to their minds.

And why not start to use this channel to boost them by saying what you genuinely like and appreciate to others while they're in earshot? This is especially useful at ages/stages when direct praise is embarrassing to them.

HEARING AND HEALING

This story is told by one of my teachers, Dr Virginia Satir.

A child had just been operated on for tonsil removal and, back in the ward, was failing to stop bleeding. Dr Satir joined the concerned staff in examining the still-open cuts in the child's throat.

On an impulse, she asked what was happening in the theatre at the time of the operation.

'Oh, we'd just finished a throat cancer operation on an old lady.'

'What were you talking about?'

'Oh, that last operation, and how she didn't have much of a chance of living – there was too much damage.'

Dr Satir's mind worked fast. She saw the child undergoing the simple and routine procedure, under general anaesthetic, while the staff talked about the previous patient: 'not much chance of living', 'pretty bad shape'.

Quickly, she asked that the child be taken back to the theatre. She instructed the staff in what to say:

'Gee, this kid looks good and healthy, not like the old lady we operated on before.' 'This kid has a nice healthy throat.' 'She'll be healed in a jiffy and back playing with her friends!'

The bleeding stopped, the anaesthetic wore off and the child went home the next day.

Adding power to our message

Scientists have realised that a message goes much deeper into a person's mind if it is accompanied by other signals that reinforce it such as touch, eye contact, or strength of voice.

This is really quite simple.

If a person says to you, 'You're a pest!', you will probably feel rather put out. If he says it with a frown and a loud voice, this will be worse.

If he says it very loudly, moves towards you whilst making menacing movements and appears somewhat out of control, then you have a problem.

If he happens to be three times larger than you and is one of your family – on whom your well-being depends – you will probably remember the incident for the rest of your life.

Modern-day men and women (especially those of Anglo-Saxon descent) tend to be constrained in our day-to-day life. We do not act or speak with very much passion or force. We tend to keep our good and bad feelings to ourselves and, when things go badly, we try to carry the burden without giving any outward signs.

Because of this, our children may live in a situation where day-to-day messages are fairly vague and indirect: 'Now don't do that, darling, come along', 'There's a good boy'. Both positive and negative messages are casual and not great in their impact.

Then, one day, when life has really overloaded Mum or Dad, there comes a powerful outburst, 'You little brat, I wish you'd shut up', accompanied with wild eyes, sudden, close proximity, ear-splitting volume and a sense of quivering lack of control that is quite unforgettable. The message is inescapable, although untrue: 'This is what Mum or Dad *really* thinks of me!'.

The words that overwrought parents choose at these times can be remarkably strong:

'I wish you'd never been born.'
'You're a stupid, stupid child.'
'You're killing me, do you hear?'
'I'd like to throttle you!'

It's not bad to get angry at or around children. On the contrary, children need to learn that one can be angry and discharge tension and be heard, in safety. Elizabeth Kubler Ross said that real anger lasts 20 seconds and is mostly noise. The problem comes when the positive messages ('You are great', 'We love you', 'We'll look after you') are not equally strong or reliable. Often, although we feel these, we do not communicate them.

Almost every child is dearly loved, but many children do not know this fact; many adults will go to their graves still believing that they were a nuisance and a disappointment to their parents. It is one of the most moving moments in family therapy to be able to clear away this misunderstanding between parent and child.

At the times when a child's life goes shaky – when a new baby is bought home, if a marriage breaks up, if failure occurs at school, or there is no work for a hopeful teenager – it is important to give positive messages, anchored with a hand on a shoulder and a clear look in the eye: whatever happens, you are special and important to us. We know you're great.

So far we've talked about the unconscious programming of children to be unhappy adults. There are lots of direct ways too!

WHAT NOT TO DO

When disciplining, don't use put-downs when a simple demand would do.

> Give that back, you selfish little brat

Don't even use put-downs in a friendly way; say, as a pet-name.

> Hey, elephants ears! Dinner's ready

Don't compare!

> You're as bad as your father

> Why can't you be sweet and good like your baby brother?

Set an example!

Never talk to other people about children's faults in their hearing.

Don't take pride in patterns that are bound to cause trouble later.

He sure belted her
He's a real little O'Reilly

Don't use guilt to control children.

These sorts of statements can be left out of your parenting repertoire for good. You and they will feel better for it.

God, you exhaust me!
I'm so sick I could just lie down and die.

Look what you're doing to your mother

How to positively program your kids

Sometimes you need to talk to your children in a direct and powerful way, looking right at them, holding them as you speak; at other times the best way is to be casual, incidental, so that they take in information easily and naturally.

It's amazing how many opportunities occur to positively program your children.

In discipline situations:

When they are having a tough time:

Just incidentally:

Tips include: don't use praise to steamroller over a child's doubts or fears. Do listen to them. Don't gush. Choose your times, and mean it. If its not true, don't pretend.

THE WAY YOU SAY IT —
POSITIVE WORDING MAKES COMPETENT KIDS

It's not only praise or put-downs that determine a child's level of confidence. We also program our kids in the way we give instructions and commands in a negative — positive choice of words.

As adults, we guide our own behaviour and feelings by 'self-talk', the chatter that goes on inside our heads. ('Better not forget to get petrol', 'Oh hell, I forgot my purse, I must be getting senile' etc.) Self-talk is learned directly from your parents and teachers. With your own kids, it's a great chance to put in all sorts of useful data, which your child can internalise — an encouraging part of themselves for life.

For example, we can say to a child, 'Don't you dare get into any fights at school today!' or we can say 'I want you to have a good time at school today and only play with the kids you like'.

Why should such a small thing make a difference? It's all in the way the human mind works. If someone offered you a million dollars not to think of a blue monkey for two minutes — you wouldn't be able to do it! (Try it now if you don't believe us!) If a child is told 'Don't fall out of the tree', then they have to think two things: 'Don't' and 'fall out of the tree'. What we think, we automatically rehearse. (Imagine biting hard into a lemon, and notice how you react just to the fantasy!) A child who is vividly imagining falling out of a tree probably will! Far better to use positive wording: 'Look for a good place to put your foot'.

There are dozens of chances each day to get this right. Rather than say '*Don't* run out into the traffic', it's easier and better to say '*Stay* on the footpath close to me, — so that the child imagines what TO do, and not what NOT to do.

Give kids clear instructions as to the right way to do things. Kids don't always know how to be safe, so make your commands specific: 'Tracey, hold onto the side of the boat with both your hands' is much more useful than 'Don't you dare fall out' or worse still 'How do you think I'll feel if you drown?'. The changes are small but the difference is enormous.

Positive wording helps your kids to think and act positively, and to feel capable in a wide range of situations. They will imagine success and talk themselves through to good outcomes. Our encouraging words will stay with them for life.

I'LL GIVE YOU CRAZY!

Have you ever listened to yourself talking to your kids, and just moaned? A lot of the things we say to kids are, well, crazy!

Scots comedian Billy Connolly bemoaned some of these in a recent concert we heard ... (you'll have to imagine the accent).

'Mum, can I go to the pictures?' 'Pictures! I'll give you pictures!'

'Can I have some bread then?' 'Bread! I'll bread you my boy!'

Most of us can remember being told things as a child which simply made no sense at all, phrases like: pull your socks up young man ... if you don't come to your senses soon ... you'll smile on the other side of your face! ... I'll teach you to make a fool of me! ... and so on. It's no wonder some people grow up to be a little confused.

Bread?
I'll bread you
my boy!

I was in a primary school recently where some parents had brought their toddlers to join in a new play group. While we were waiting to start, a lively and curious little boy started to pull out some maths equipment from a shelf. His harassed looking mum told him 'If you touch that the teacher will cut your fingers off!' Now any of us can understand the motivation to say this kind of thing — when nothing else works, try terror! But with this kind of message coming thick and fast, what can a child conclude about life? It can only go two ways: either the world is a crazy and dangerous place, or else, it's no good listening to Mum, she talks a load of rubbish. Now there's the start of a well-adjusted life!

One day (true confession) I told my two-year-old son that the police might be cross with him if he didn't wear his seatbelt. I was hot and tired, and I hate squirming my six-foot-four frame around inside cars to fasten seatbelt buckles on protesting kids. I resorted to a cheap trick, and I paid the price. As soon as the words came out of my mouth I regretted it. For days after I had questions thick and fast. 'Do the policeman have guns?' 'Are there any policeman down this road?' It was a major job of rehabilitation to get him back to feeling calm and comfortable about the men and women in blue.

We don't always have to explain everything to our kids, or endlessly reason with them till we are blue in the face. 'Because I say so' is a good enough reason some of the time. But there is nothing ever to be gained by needlessly scaring them. 'When your father gets home ...' 'You'll make me so sick I'll have to go away ...' 'We'll put you into a home ...' are the kind of messages that harm and haunt even tough children. We are their main source of information early on, and later our credibility is put to the test (since they have or will have other sources to compare us with). Our job is to give them a realistic, even slightly rosy picture of the world – which they can build on as they go, and so become hardy and secure on the inside. When they encounter trickiness or dishonesty later in life, they will at least know that this isn't completely the way of the world, that some people are trustworthy, and safe to be around – Mum and Dad included.

Why do parents put children down?

At this point in the book, you could be feeling guilty about the way that you speak to your own children. Please don't – it isn't too late to change. There is plenty you can do to overcome old programming whether your children are still little or even if they are now adults.

The first step is to begin understanding yourself, to know why put-downs became part of your parenting in the first place. Almost every parent uses unnecessary put-downs from time to time. There are three main reasons for this.

1. You repeat what was said to you!

You weren't taught about parenting in school. But you did have one clear example to work from – your own parents.

I'm sure you've found yourself in a heated moment yelling at your kids and then thinking, 'Good grief, that's what my parents used to say to me and I hated it!'. Those old tape recordings are your 'automatic pilot', however, and it takes presence of mind to stop yourself and say something else.

Some parents, of course, go to the other extreme. With painful memories of the way in which they were raised, they swear never to scold, hit or deprive their own children. The danger here is that they may overdo it, and their children suffer from a lack of control. It isn't easy, is it?

2. You just thought it was the right thing to do!

It was once thought that kids were basically bad, and the thing to do was to tell them how bad they were. This would shame them into being better!

Perhaps you were brought up in this way. As a parent you simply hadn't thought about self-esteem or the need to help children gain confidence. If so, I hope that what you are reading has changed your mind. Now that you realise how put-downs damage children, I'm sure you'll be keen to stop using them.

3. You are 'stressed out'

When money is short, or you are overworked, lonely or bored, then you are much more likely to be destructive in what you say to kids.

The reasons for this are clear. When we are pressured in any way, we build up a body tension which needs discharging. It actually does feel good to lash out at someone, in words or actions.

Our children often cop it because they are easier to get angry with than our spouse, boss, landlord, or whomever. It's important to think it through: I feel so tense! Who am I *really* angry with?

The relief of lashing out is short-lived since the child is likely to behave even more badly as a result, but at the time it feels like a release.

If this happens, it is vitally important that you find a safe way to let off steam.

Tension can be released in two ways:

1. By vigorous action, such as hitting a mattress, doing some vigorous work, going for a brisk walk. This is no small matter – many a child's life has been saved by being shut in its bedroom while a distraught parent walks around the block as a means of calming down;
2. By dissolving the stress through talking with a friend, finding affection from a partner (if you're fortunate enough to have one) or through some activity such as yoga, sport or massage that releases the stress and allows your body to relax deeply.

Eventually as a mum or dad, you must learn to care for yourself as much as for your children. You actually do more for your kids by spending some time each day on your own (health and relaxation) than by being totally devoted to serving them every second of the day. (More about this in Chapter 8.)

So, that's the end of the bad news. The rest of this book is about how to do it the easier way! It is possible to change, and many parents have told me that just hearing about these ideas at a meeting or on the radio has helped them immediately.

Already while you've been reading, your ideas have been changing. You'll find that, without even trying, your behaviour with your children will start to be easier and more positive. I promise!

2
What children really want

It's cheaper than video games, and healthier than ice-cream!

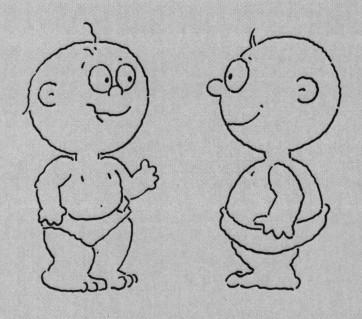

The question that is uppermost in the minds of millions of parents everyday can be summed up in one word ...

Why do kids play up? Why do they always explore where they shouldn't? Why do they do things that they are not supposed to – fight, tease, disobey, provoke, argue, make a mess, and generally seem to want to persecute Mum and Dad?

Why do some kids actually seem to *enjoy* getting into trouble?

This chapter tells you what is going on inside 'naughty' children, and how 'bad' behaviour is actually the result of good (healthy)forces going astray.

After reading this chapter, you'll be able to see more sense in children's misbehaviour and you'll also know how to prevent and divert it to happier alternatives.

You don't believe me? Read on!

Children play up for one reason only: they have *unmet needs*. 'But what needs,' you are thinking, 'do my children have that are unmet? I feed them, clothe them, buy them toys, keep them warm and clean ... '

Well, there are some extra needs (luckily very cheap to provide) which go beyond the 'basics' mentioned. These mysterious needs are essential, not only to make happy children but to maintain life itself. Perhaps I can explain best by telling a story.

In 1945, the Second World War ended and Europe lay in ruins. Among the many human problems to be tackled was that of caring for the thousands of orphans whose parents had been killed or permanently separated from them by the war.

The Swiss, who had managed to stay out of the war itself, sent their health workers out to begin tackling some of these problems; one man, a doctor, was given the job of researching how to best care for the orphan babies.

He travelled about Europe and visited many kinds of orphan-care situations, to see what was the most successful type of care. He saw many extremes. In some places, American field hospitals had been set up and the babies were snug in stainless steel cots, in hygienic wards, getting their four-hourly feeds of special milk formula from crisply uniformed nurses.

At the other end of the scale, in remote mountain villages, a truck had simply pulled up, the driver had asked, 'Can you look after these babies?' and left half-a-dozen crying infants in the care of the villagers. Here, surrounded by kids, dogs, goats, in the arms of the village women, the babies took their chances on goats' milk and the communal stewpot.

The Swiss doctor had a simple way of comparing the different forms of care. No need even to weigh the babies, far less measure coordination or look for smiling and eye contact. In those days of influenza and dysentery he used the simplest of all statistics – the death rate.

And what he discovered was rather a surprise ... As epidemics raged through Europe and many people were dying, the children in the rough villages were thriving better than their scientifically-cared-for counterparts in the hospitals!

The doctor had discovered something that old wives had known for a long time. He had discovered that babies need *love* to live.

The infants in the field hospital had everything but affection and stimulation. The babies in the villages had more hugs, bounces and things to see than they knew what to do with and, given reasonable basic care, were thriving

Of course, the doctor didn't use the word 'love' (words like that upset scientists) but he spelt it out clearly enough. What was important, he said, was:

- skin-to-skin contact frequently, and from two or three special people;
- movement of a gentle but robust kind, such as carrying around, bouncing on a knee, and so on;
- eye contact, smiling, and a colourful, lively environment;
- sounds such as singing, talking, goo-gooing, and so on.

It was an important discovery, and the first time that it had been stated scientifically. Babies need human contact and affection (and not just to be fed, warmed and cleaned). If they are not given these human ingredients, they may easily die.

So much for babies. But what about older children?

Here is an interesting thing – it's a graph of my estimate of the amount of touching (that's right, physical touching) that people receive as their lives unfold.

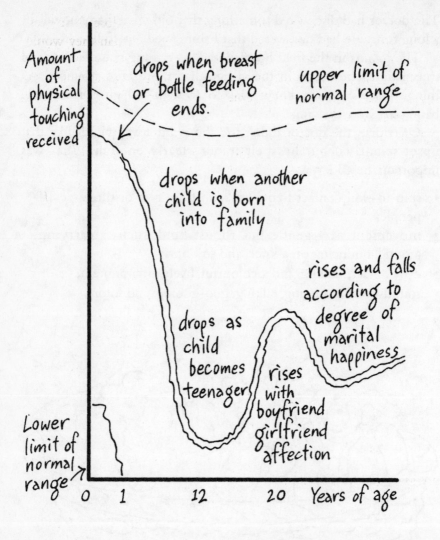

Amount of physical touching received

drops when breast or bottle feeding ends.

upper limit of normal range

drops when another child is born into family

rises and falls according to degree of marital happiness

drops as child becomes teenager

rises with boyfriend girlfriend affection

Lower limit of normal range

0   1   12   20   Years of age

Remember, this is the average situation. Who knows what is the ideal – perhaps a line straight across. You may be wondering about the dip at about two to three years of age. That's when child number two (or three or four) usually comes along and affection has to be shared – a rough time for everyone!

Little babies like to be touched and cuddled. So do small children, although they are choosier about who does the cuddling. Teenagers often get awkward about it, but will admit in trust that they like affection as much as anyone. And, of course, by late teens they are pursuing specialised forms of affection with great energy!

I once asked an audience of about 60 adults to close their eyes, and then raise their hands if they got less affection than they would like to get in daily life. It was unanimous – every hand went up. After a minute the peeping began and the room began to ring with laughter. From this careful scientific study, I conclude that adults need affection, too!

Apart from physical touch, we find other ways to get good feelings from people. The most obvious one is by using words.

We all need to be recognised, noticed and, preferably, given sincere praise. We want to be included in conversations, have our ideas listened to and even admired.

A three-year-old says it out straight: 'Look at me'.

Most rich people take very little pleasure in their bank balance unless it can be displayed and someone is there to notice.

I often have a good chuckle to myself with the thought that most of the adult world is made up of big three-year-olds running about shouting, 'Look at me, Daddy', 'Watch me, you guys'. Not me, of course – I give lectures and write books out of mature adult concern!

So, an interesting picture emerges. We take care of our children's bodily needs but, if this is all we do, they still miss out. They have psychological needs, too, and these are simple but essential. A child needs stimulation of a human kind. (It isn't enough to plonk them in front of a TV set.) They must have a diet of talking each day, with some affection and praise added in, in order to be happy. If this is given fully, and not begrudgingly from behind a pile of ironing or a newspaper, then it will not even take very long!

Many people reading this will have older children, or teenagers. You may be thinking, 'But already they have learned some bad ways of getting attention. How can I deal with that?'.

Here is another story.

'OF MICE AND MEN'

A few years ago, psychologists got about in white coats and worked mostly with rats. (Nowadays they wear tweed jackets and work mostly with young women – things are looking up!) The 'rat psychologists' were able to learn a lot about behaviour because they could do things with rats that they couldn't with children. Read on, and you'll see what I mean.

In one particular experiment, rats were placed in a special cage, with food and drink, and a little lever. They ate, drank and ran about, and eventually asked themselves the same question you are asking: 'What's the little lever for?'. They pressed it (being like children, they wanted to try everything) and, to their surprise, a little window opened in the cage to reveal a film being shown on the wall outside. Perhaps it was Mickey Mouse – I don't know! The window soon closed and the rat had to press the lever again to get more of the movie.

The rats were willing to work very hard at lever-pressing to keep the movie in view, leading us to *principle one*: intelligent creatures, like rats (and children), like to have something interesting to do. This helps their brains to grow.

The researchers then put the rats in a different cage, with food and drink but no lever and no window. The rats were content for a little while but then started misbehaving! They chewed the walls, fought with each other, rubbed their fur off, and were generally bad rats! This leads us to *principle two*: intelligent creatures, like rats (and children), will do anything to keep from being bored including things we could call silly or destructive.

Finally, the researchers really got nasty. They tried a cage with food and drink, and with little wires placed across the floor and attached to a battery. Every now and then a shock was sent through the wires, enough to give the little creatures a real start but not to injure them. (You see now why they didn't use children.)

Finally, the exciting moment arrived. The rats were taken out of the cages and given a choice of which they would prefer to go back into. Perhaps you, the reader, could make a guess as to which was the rats' first choice, second choice, and so on? Here they are again:

- cage with food, drink and movies;
- cage with food and drink;
- cage with food, drink and unexpected shocks.

Have you guessed? Well, the rats preferred the movies best of all. If you didn't guess that one . . . back to the start of the book! The second choice was the really interesting one: they preferred the cage with shocks to the one with only food and drink. This leads us to *principle three*, an important principle indeed for children: intelligent creatures, like rats (and children), would rather have bad things happening than nothing at all.

Or, in other words, any stimulation or excitement is better than none even if it's somewhat painful.

In child terms, if a child has to choose between being ignored and being scolded or even smacked, which do you think he'll prefer? Which do your children choose? Of course, if positive attention is available, at least once or twice a day, then neither of the above will be so appealing.

I'll conclude this section with one more story – this time about children. You are smarter than children or rats so it won't need any explaining!

An up-and-coming young couple had two boys, aged nine and eleven.

The boys had a playroom under the house with a billiard table, a refrigerator full of soft drinks, a record player (video games hadn't been invented at that stage, or they would have had one of those, too) and so on. However, the parents found that, despite the facilities provided, the boys were always fighting; it was even embarrassing to have guests for dinner. They finally took the boys to a behavioural clinic to seek the help of psychologists. The psychologists said to the parents, 'Well, we mostly know about rats, but we're willing to come over and have a look'. The arrangements were made. The parents thought it a little odd, but were keen to solve the problem that was badly affecting their social life.

The psychologists came in a team and installed themselves around the house with notepads and stopwatches. It was the evening of a cocktail party, so some of the psychologists stayed upstairs (where the adults were) and some were with the boys downstairs (sitting silently taking detailed notes). At about 7 o'clock the upstairs observers noted the mother glancing downwards and then across at her husband. Simultaneously, the observers downstairs had noted that the boys, having played with the various games and toys, had begun to fight. The fighting was rather unusual, though – it had more the look of a stage fight or a kind of a dance. The noise, however, was very fight-like!

The observers in the basement then saw the father appear on the stairs and, having been told by the psychologists to act normally (not an easy thing to do) begin to berate the boys for being disruptive. The psychologists scribbled furiously: they had noticed a unique thing, something they had never seen in rats. The boys listened to their father shouting and looked suitably chastised, except for a small and curious twist about the mouth – an expression which has become famous. Psychologists call it 'the Mona Lisa smile' ...

Child psychologists now realise that this half-smile is a secret message, which means, 'Well, I should be feeling bad, and I'm trying hard to look remorseful but, you know, I'm kind of enjoying this!'. Parents have never really figured this out but they react to it unknowingly with that famous parent sentence, 'Wipe that smile off your face when I'm talking to you!'.

Meanwhile, back in the basement, the boys were getting more attention from Dad than they had received all day and had to struggle hard not to show their pleasure.

The psychologists went back to their laboratory, prepared a detailed report and met with the parents to tell them what you have probably already guessed: 'You're too busy with your social life; the boys need more attention. They like their Dad because boys of this age want to learn how to be a man, and so they have found the one thing that they know will bring their Dad into the picture: fighting'.

The psychologists were right, but they didn't understand the parents very well. The parents' reply was, 'What a load of rubbish. How could children possibly like being told off?'. The parents, you see, didn't know about the rats and the electric shocks, let alone the Mona Lisa smile.

The parents took their boys off to a psychiatrist, who analysed their dreams for two years, then gave up and took them playing golf with him, which of course cured them!

We can easily summarise the above:

Children play up because they're bored.

Is there something you could do to give them more stimulation – go to the park with a ball, have their friends over, join a play group, get toys from a toy library, have a box of bits and pieces for imaginary play so that they, and you, don't feel 'caged in'?

Children play up because they feel unwanted.

Can you spend a little time each day giving full, positive attention and physical contact? And are you relaxed and happy enough to give *them* a secure feeling?

Children play up because it gets them noticed.

Watch for the Mona Lisa smile, a sign that some attention is needed for doing the *right* thing.

TALKING IS BRAIN-FOOD FOR KIDS ...

By the time they reach school age, some kids can talk very well and have a wide vocabulary. Some on the other hand are very limited in their verbal skills. This can be a real disadvantage – for one thing, teachers often use talking skills as an indicator of intelligence and ability, and so your kids can be either deliberately, or unconsciously, labelled as 'slow'.

How can you help your kids to be good with words? And why the differences?

It was found as early as the 1950s that parents fall into two distinct groups in their approaches to talking to children. Some people are very abrupt and brief in what they say to their kids:

'Dwayne, shut that bleeding door!', 'Get here!', 'Eat it!' and so on. Others were the opposite: 'Charles sweetheart, would you mind closing the door – it's blowing quite a draught on little Sebastian, there's a good boy!'.

You don't have to be a professor to see that young Charles is going to have more words in his head than little Dwayne, and more ways of stringing them together. (Though on the other hand Dwayne may also know some words that Charles doesn't!)

Most parents today talk to their children, explaining things and just chatting to them for the pleasure of it. Even babies enjoy being chatted to, and toddlers understand much more than they let on.

Here are the basic steps:

1. DURING PREGNANCY make lots of sounds to and around your baby. You can start by singing or crooning when you feel like it, having music playing (quite loudly is fine). If you're a Dad, snuggle up and talk to the baby! This way your child will come to know and feel safe with your manly voice and be easier for you to comfort when they are little. Repetition and familiarity helps – the sound of TV's *Days of Our Lives* theme music has been found to soothe newborns who 'listened' to it with Mum during pregnancy!

2. WITH INFANTS continue all this talk, singing, and music exposure once the baby is born. Moving or swinging them about will add to their delight and sense of rhythm, which is a necessary part of speech. (Special high-speed movies have been taken which show that we all do a subtle swaying dance as we speak – that it is almost impossible to be still while speaking.) If you can carry the

babe about with you in a sling or harness as you work, all the better. As you go through the day with toddlers, tell them about what you are doing, using simple words, but not all baby talk. Use repetition of those words they say to you, so as to polish up what they are saying.

3. AS THE TODDLERS START TO TALK MORE you can help by echoing and adding to what they say to you, so they are both encouraged by the response, and helped to get the words right.

'Buppa!', 'You want the butter?', 'Want buppa!'

and a little later:

'Pass butta ayy?', 'You want me to pass the butter?', 'Pass me butter!' and so on!

Do all this casually – as a game – with no undue pressure or expectations.

A recent TV series featured interviews with 'superbright' or 'hothouse' kids. It gave us some mixed feelings – these kids were certainly high achievers, but some by adulthood had turned into real oddballs! One family though stood out – for the naturalness and balance of their kids. All four daughters ranging from eight to sixteen were friendly, relaxed, very down-to-earth, and yet extraordinarily advanced in their skills. The sixteen-year-old for instance had simply skipped primary school (at her teacher's suggestion – the parents had been quite happy for her to go). She was now doing doctoral research into spinal cell damage. Asked how they had raised such genius kids, the father said 'It couldn't be genetic – I haven't had the sperm bank knocking on my door!'. (And he did look, well, rather ordinary!) The mother added that 'We just explain to them …' She explained that as she vacuumed the house, for example, she would tell the baby she was carrying on her back about what she was doing, that the noise was made by the motor inside the vacuum cleaner, which was electrical and turned very fast, that the air it blew through made a lot of noise, and so on …

One could imagine her manner being cheerful and natural – not 'schoolmarmish', giving stern lectures, but rather 'Hey, this is interesting!'. If you find car trips or shopping with little children rather boring at times, then perhaps this kind of chatter will make it more fun for both of you.

In our family we've gone onto the next problem now – how to stop a four-year-old from talking ALL THE TIME! But at least she does it well!

FATHERING – DOING THINGS TOGETHER

When our son was small we lived on a quiet country lane, half a kilometre from the post office and general store. It was a nice walk to get the mail, on a sunny morning, and took ten minutes there and back. Unless you took a two-year-old! Two-year-old kids do not think like adults – they do not know the meaning of 'long term goals'. They don't even have 'application to the task in hand'. Anything but. Each step of the way has to be the subject of intense negotiations! 'I wanna play inna green water!'

Once, out of dedication to science, I tried something out. I completely gave in, and let 'the kid' investigate every drain, ditch, dead worm, puddle and rock that he wanted to, along the way. (If early influences determine eventual careers – my son will be something big in sewerage.) Anyhow, to cut a (very) long story short, it took two and a half hours! After a while, I even started to enjoy it!

It's very clear from everything we know about families, that kids – especially boys – get a lot out of being around fathers. Something different and complementary to what mothers provide takes place at these times. And for the most part, being with fathers means 'doing things together'. It's not like in all the movies and shows like *The Waltons*. In the Waltons family they sit down, and have 'heart-to-heart talks'. Maybe this happens in the good old U.S. of A. (and good luck to them) but in Australia people go kind of catatonic if they are sat face to face like that. Of the adults I spoke to, those who got on well with their Dads did some talking and listening – but it was carefully concealed amidst activity. Trust and self disclosure grow gradually – while on the surface we are just loading the wood, working on the car, rounding up the sheep.

You'll notice some of these are rural pursuits. The city doesn't lend itself quite as much to doing things together – not so actively anyway. You can only take out the garbage so many times! City parents I talk to seem to get close to their kids while taxi-driving them between activities like athletics to ballet and back to piano. This is the time to actually ask how they are going, and draw them out a little, though you have to time it to the trip.

For fathers, doing stuff with your kids is vital. It allows closeness to just happen. Conversations wander into deeper realms. Things just kind of pop out unguarded, and an easygoing father can actually influence the direction of his own kids' lives – much better than leaving this all to Hollywood and peer groups.

When doing things with your children, some simple rules apply:

1. DON'T EXPECT TO ACTUALLY ACHIEVE ANYTHING! Especially with small children (like going to the post office) the goal is no longer the goal. For example – if you are teaching them to use a screwdriver, you won't get the door hung in a great hurry. So let go of that one. They'll wander off in a while and you can make up for lost time.

2. ONLY DO THINGS WITH KIDS WHICH YOU FEEL RELAXED ABOUT. Their help in planting out spring seedlings will not give you an immaculate garden. You have to decide what you are doing – being with your kids, or getting the job done to your usual standards. If you try to do both you will experience a little frustration. Settle for sweeping up *some* of the leaves, but mainly having fun together. That way they will see 'gardening with Dad' as a fun activity, and ten years later will volunteer to mow the lawn!

3. ENJOY PARENTHOOD – IT DOESN'T LAST! I was in my thirties when my son arrived, and so am mindful of parenthood being all too short. If he wanders by when I'm doing a job, I value the contact with him and like to see what I can teach him there and then. But not when I'm writing on the computer!

In conclusion – as a father you need to decide moment to moment what is more important to you, and it will sometimes be the kids, and sometimes not. One big plus is that kids tend to slow you down, and while slowed down, you start to rediscover little pleasures, which is the gift they bring. Time with kids is never wasted.

3
Curing by listening

How to help youngsters deal with an unkind world.

Your child is upset. Something has gone wrong at school or with another child or adult, and you don't know how to help. You would like your child to find a way of dealing with the problem so he or she will be less vulnerable. This chapter will show you how to help.

The world is sometimes an unfair and difficult place for kids and, much as we would like to, we parents can't smooth out all the bumps. In fact, we shouldn't, since it's through dealing with difficult people and situations that our children become mature and independent adults.

We'll look firstly at what *not* to say to kids when life is treating them badly: the kinds of statements that can put a wall between you and your child. Then you'll learn of a remarkable skill called 'active listening', which parents are finding is the most positive way they can help kids deal with life.

Since we are their 'safe harbour', children often bring problems to us to see if we can help. The way that we react to these calls for help will either open up greater trust or put up a barrier that will be hard to take down. There are three ways that parents typically react, that cause the barriers to go up:

Patronising
'Oh, you poor thing.
Here, let me fix it for you.'

Lecturing
'Well, you are stupid to have got into this mess, so I'll tell you what to do. Now, listen carefully to me ...'

Distracting

'Oh well, never mind let's go and play crick

Which is your style? Do you rush to the rescue, or give wise advice, change the subject?

Let's take a closer look at each of these three styles.

Patronising

'How was your day?'

'Bad!'

'Oh, you poor thing. Come and tell me all about it.'

'We had this new teacher for maths. And I couldn't keep up.'

'Well, that's really awful. Do you want me to help you with the work after tea?'

'I didn't bring it home.'

'Perhaps I could ring the school tomorrow and talk to the principal?'

'Oh, well; I dunno …'

'I think it's best to get to the bottom of things before it gets worse, don't you?'

Well, err … mmm.'

'I wouldn't want your education to suffer.'

'Uh-huh.'

Lecturing

'How was your day?'

'Bad!'

'Well, you're a fine one to complain. I'd love to be able to spend my day learning, having a nice easy time.'

'Well, we had a hard time. We've got this stupid new maths teacher ...'

'Now don't you go talking about your teachers in that tone. If you paid a bit more attention you'd be better off, my boy. You think you should have everything on a plate!'

'Hmmm.'

Distracting

'How was your day?'

'Bad!'

'Oh, come on, it wasn't that bad was it? Have a sandwich?'

'Thanks. I'm a bit worried about maths ...'

'Well. You're no Einstein, but neither are your Mum 'n' Dad. You go and put the TV on and don't let it get you down ...'

'Uh-huh.'

You'll notice in all three examples the same thing happens: the parent does all the talking; the conversation stops pretty soon; the child doesn't get to talk over the real problem. The child's feelings get lost along the way; the parent 'solves' the problem – or thinks he has; the child says less and less.

Now look at a different approach ...

Active listening

'How was your day?'

'Bad!'

'You look really unhappy. What went wrong?'

'Aw, we've got a new teacher for maths. He goes too fast.'

'You're worried you won't be able to keep up?'

'Yes. I asked him to explain part of it and he said just to pay more attention.'

'Hmmm ... How did you feel about that?'

'Really wild – the other kids all stirred me ... but they're having trouble, too!'

'So you're angry that you got into trouble because you piped up first?'

'Yes, I don't like getting shown up in front of everyone.'

'What do you think you'll do?'

'I'm not sure, I suppose I could ask him again, when the class is over.'

'You think that would work better?'

'Yes, then I wouldn't feel so embarrassed. And I think he's a bit nervous, too. Maybe that's why he rushes.'

'You can understand it from his point of view?'

'Yeah, I reckon he's just nervous of us.'

'No wonder, teaching such smart kids like you!'

'Yeah!'

This, then, is active listening. In such cases parents are far from silent: they are interested, and show it by confirming their child's feelings and thoughts and by helping the child to think it through. Using this approach:

- parents rarely give remedies or attempt to rescue ('I'll call the school') – unless this is clearly necessary;
- they rarely advise ('You should ask for help') – unless the child really needs information;
- they rarely distract the child from the problem ('Oh well, have a sandwich') – unless the child is a chronic whinger!

The skill of active listening takes some practice to acquire, and is taught in classes called 'Parent Effectiveness Training' around Australia. It is also explained in the book of the same name by Dr Thomas Gordon (see *References*, p. 136).

Many parents have found active listening a great relief. They don't have to keep their child forever happy and they don't have to solve the child's problems for him. With active listening they can help the child, while leaving the responsibility, and pleasure, of a solution to the child. The trick is to ask yourself, 'Could my child benefit, in the long run, from solving this problem himself?' You can offer time, clarity and understanding so that a problem can be turned into a learning experience.

Sometimes parents must intervene, as the following story illustrates.

A friend of mine has a nine-year-old son who broke his leg and needed a plaster for some weeks. When the plaster was removed he was naturally shaky on his feet for a while. A physical education teacher at the primary school he attended had the class run round the oval and my friend's son came last, an embarrassment to him because he was a good runner. The teacher, without waiting for an explanation, made the boy run the oval again, but this time in his underwear only and in front of the rest of the class.

When the boy arrived home in tears and his parents learned of what had happened, they were so angry that they saw the school principal the same night and asked that the teacher be dismissed. The teacher was, in fact, transferred to another school, where we can only hope the same does not happen again.

This is a case in which parents must become involved and defend their children's rights because the children are powerless to defend themselves. In some cases, kids do NOT want our help – just our support. To get involved would be the wrong thing . . .

'Just listening' is powerful medicine. If we can hold back from putting instant band-aids on every hurt, we can enter the deeper world of our children.

Mandy, aged six, was in a bad mood. In fact, she had been out of sorts for a few weeks. She was more argumentative with her younger brother and had started not wanting to go to kinder in the mornings. Her mother decided to use 'active listening' to see if she could find the trouble. She asked Mandy, 'You look sad. Do you want to tell me about it?'. Mandy came and sat on her lap but didn't talk much.

Next day, Mandy had to be stopped from fighting with her baby brother and was put in her room for a few minutes to cool off. Later that night, Dad commented, 'You seem kind of cross at the moment'.

Mandy gave one piercing look at her Mum and burst into tears. 'They call me Yuk Face.' In the next ten minutes or so Mandy moved through anger and tears in succession, while her Mum resisted the urge to distract her or try and cheer her up. Mandy did indeed have a scar on her face, which one day would be healed with surgery, but for a while she would have to live with it.

When she had let out some of the bad feelings she'd collected from children at school, Mandy was much more peaceful. 'I'm not yucky, am I, Mummy?' Nope! You're terrific!

Sometimes children want you to do something – in which case they should ask straight out.

Jonathan, aged fourteen, hung around the kitchen for ages, looking very awkward. Finally he told Mum, with some embarrassment, that an older girl had asked him to go to a motel for the night with her! His Mum had to battle hard not to start laying down the law. She said instead, 'Gee, what do you think you'll do? You sound like you're feeling pretty unsure'. 'Well, I don't know. Mum, would you forbid me to go? Please?'

Jonathan's Mum was very happy to forbid him to go. Jonathan was most relieved: he saved face at school and with the girl. Jonathan's mother told me later that she would have forbidden him to go but wanted him to make his decision, too. A brave lady!

4

Kids and emotions

What is really going on?

This is probably a good place to make a confession. The title of this book *The Secret of Happy Children* is a little idealistic!

In the adult world, no-one is ever, or would want to be, continually happy. So for our children, such an aim actually would be wrong. If you try to make kids happy all the time, you will actually make them and yourself quite miserable! What we really want is kids who can handle and move along through the many feelings that life brings . . . Joy is the goal, but being comfortable and experiencing all the emotions life brings is the way to get there most often.

A proper understanding of emotions has been missing in our culture until recently. We've only just escaped from the era of 'big boys don't cry', and 'it's not ladylike to get angry'. Few areas of understanding are as needed and helpful right now as getting back in touch with how feelings work. Luckily, the 'facts about feelings' are now available to help both us, and our kids, to find the inner peace and vitality that make up emotional health.

What do we mean by emotions?

Emotions are distinctive sets of body sensations, which we experience under specific situations. They range in intensity from subtle to incredibly strong. They are constantly with us – flowing and merging together as we resolve each event in our life and move on. *We are always feeling something* – emotions are a symptom of being alive!

There are four basic emotions – *anger, fear, sadness* and *joy*. All other shades of feeling are a mix of these – like colours mixed from the primaries red, yellow and blue. There are thousands of combinations possible – like jealousy – a mixture of anger and fear; or nostalgia – a mixture of joy and sadness! We are such interesting creatures!

When our children are newly born, their emotions are only just beginning to take shape. Observant parents can watch babies in the early months developing separate and distinct expressions of how they are feeling – the shriek of fear, the tears of sadness, red-faced rage, and chortles of joy.

Infants are not inhibited – they *express* feelings naturally and easily, and as a result the negative emotions soon pass. However a growing child has to *learn* how to deal with feelings socially, and find constructive outlets for the powerful energy that feelings create. A child depends on us as parents for this information – luckily it isn't too hard to get this right – as we'll show.

Understanding emotions — why we have them, how they can be best expressed, what to avoid — this is the key to a happier life with children.

Why do we have emotions?

Sometimes you could almost wish you had no feelings. Especially the negative ones like anger or sadness, which cause so much pain. Why then did nature equip us with these highly charged states? Each has a big role to play — as you'll see.

Take anger first. Imagine a person who for some reason never feels anger. Somehow they were raised without a cross bone in their body! They are standing one day in the shopping centre car park. A car drives up and parks right on their foot! Our super-accepting person would just stand there waiting until the driver did their shopping and came back!

... afraid I may have dented your wheel!

Anger is what makes us stand up for ourselves. Without it we would be slaves, doormats, mice! Anger is our instinct for freedom and self-preservation.

Fear is of definite value too. Why else do you drive on the correct side of the road? Fear keeps you from taking high risks. If you don't believe fear is useful, recall the times when you've been in a car with a driver who seems to have no fear! Fear slows us down, forces us to stop, think and avoid danger – even when our conscious brain has not yet fathomed what that danger might be.

Sadness is the emotion that helps us to grieve – it literally washes us clean of the distress of losing something or someone from our life. The chemical changes which go with sadness help our brain to release the pain, and so move on to new life. Only by being sad can we 'let go' and so make new contact with people and life.

So you can see that, properly handled,

anger .... keeps us free

fear .... keeps us safe

sadness .... keeps us in contact with people and the world

All three of these outcomes are central to our happiness. Joy, the fourth emotion, is what we experience when these needs (freedom, safety and contact) are fulfilled.

Teaching kids about anger

You can teach your kids specifically how to understand and handle each of the three 'negative' emotions. Let's take anger first.

The immediate impulse that children have when they are angry is to hit out. This has a natural purpose, but must be modified somewhat if we are to get along in the world.

Whenever we intervene with children, our aim should be to help them learn what will work and serve them well as adults. Think for a moment – what is an ideal way for an adult to handle anger? It comes down to a balance. A person who is being mistreated in some way needs to be able to say so out loud, with conviction, and to do so early on (before they feel or act violent.) Anger and violence are not the same thing. Violence is anger gone wrong.

An adult learns to moderate their anger so that it has impact, but does not do damage or become abusive. If our child shows too little anger, they may be seen as a wimp, and be pushed around or used by other kids. Too much anger makes them unpopular or even a bully. Getting this balance right is what our kids need to learn about – and it takes a few years of practice, starting from toddler age on.

SURVEY – ASSESSING YOUR CHILD'S 'EMOTIONAL LITERACY'

Name of child

_____

Position in family

_____

Able to express anger

0 not at all | **1** only by tantrums, acting out, aggression | **2** strongly and able to say they are angry, in words, safely | ☐

Able to express sadness

0 not at all | **1** only by converting it to anger or sulking | **2** able to say they are sad, cry, get a hug | ☐

Able to express fear

0 not at all | **1** only by hitting out, attacking or withdrawing | **2** able to speak fears out loud, talk them over | ☐

Able to express happiness

0 not at all | **1** only by acting 'stupid', thoughtless or agitated | **2** able to say they are happy, dance and sing, hug and laugh | ☐

If you like, you can add these up to give an emotional literacy score out of 8. Six or less needs work! ☐

If you can see where your child is having trouble, you can encourage and help them to talk through what they are really feeling and why. They can do drawings if they are young. Toddlers can point to the drawings of faces to tell you what they are feeling. This takes a lot of gentleness and care. Perhaps you too can work on expressing feelings and show your child by your own example how to be emotionally honest and expressive in safe ways.

To help kids be comfortable with anger

1. Insist that they use words instead of actions to express anger. They have to say out loud that they are angry, and if possible why.

2. Help them to connect their feelings with reasons. Talk with them to check out what is behind their outburst. Young kids will sometimes need help to 'think back' to what went wrong.
   'Are you angry with Josh because he took your truck?'
   'Did you get sick of waiting for me to finish talking?'
   Soon they will be able to tell you what is wrong and why – instead of going straight to impulsive actions.

3. Let them know that feelings are heard, and accepted (but may not always change things).
   'You've got a right to be angry with me. I wasn't listening. I'm listening now.'
   or
   'I know you're tired of waiting in this shop, and so am I, but that's just how it is. What can you do to feel better instead of hassling your brother?'

4. Teach directly that hitting is not an acceptable way to handle anger. Confront this directly, give a negative consequence for each and every hitting instance, and insist that a child do what they should have done in the first place (usually USE WORDS)!

5. Help children to say what they DO want. Often they will start to whine and complain about what they don't want. They need your help to be more positive . . .
   'He hits me.'
   'Tell him very loud not to do that.'

   'Myra took my bike.'
   'Go and ask her if you can have it back now. Tell her it's yours and you want it.'

6. Show them by your own example. When it's all added up, they are more likely to do what you DO, than what you SAY. So be sure to role model what you want. When YOU are angry, say so, in a loud voice. Get angry and be loud early, before you are REALLY steamed up. Once it is dealt with, let go, so they will learn that anger can be expressed, and then is gone. Simply say the words often and easily:

'I'm angry!'
'You're crowding me!'
'Stop interrupting!'
'I'm annoyed that you didn't keep our deal. What's going on?'

Kids learn far better about anger from a parent who is moderately expressive, than one who is always sweet, reasonable and contained. Kids need to see that parents are human too.

You can be very angry with kids without ever using abuse, or put-downs. Just stick to the direct expression of feelings and reasons. For kids, getting anger right takes a while. Be happy if your children are showing SOME signs of restraint – you will see them holding back from hitting another child or you, or saying out loud 'I'm angry'. Many adults haven't learned these lessons yet, so you are making good progress.

Teaching kids about sadness

There has always been a folklore understanding of sadness – that it's good to have a cry when things become too much. Fighting against this has been the strait-laced Victorian notion of the stiff upper lip, of 'being a man' or 'being strong'. Also in everyday usage amongst kids is the idea that you can cry too much, and that to do so is a bit suspect – there's a special name for this, being a 'sook'.

To cry sometimes is as necessary and as natural as breathing. Far from making you strong, not crying actually makes you uptight, you tend to live in the past and be hard to contact in the present, and fearful of other people's emotions or anything associated with death or loss. If you know how to cry and release sadness, you know you can handle anything.

Scientists have found that when a person cries, their body releases chemicals of the endorphin family, which block pain receptors, and produce a healing anaesthesia through the worst of the anguish that loss sometimes brings. This chemical is present even in our tears themselves. It's closely related to, and as powerful as, morphine.

To help kids be comfortable with sadness
Sadness follows its own course as long as we provide support and understanding. All we need to do is be present, calm ourselves down as we sit or stand with a child who cries. Sometimes they will want to press against us and be held, other times they will want to be separate.

If it feels right, you can give permission: 'It's okay to cry', 'It's really sad about Grandpa', 'I'm sad too'. You can explain slightly if a child is confused or awkward: 'Tony was a good friend of yours. He's worth feeling sad about'.

We once were at a friend's place. We were watching a great video movie called *Mask*. It had just ended, and everyone was enjoying being sad, in fact our hostess was sobbing loudly. Her three-year-old appeared at the door in pyjamas, came over to Mum, put out a tender hand, and said 'It's okay, let it all out!'.

Helping children handle fear

Fear is something we all need. It's vitally important that children learn to freeze, and stop from running into danger. Also we want to know that they can run or jump quickly to avoid being hurt by a speeding car or a bicycle veering their way on the footpath going to school. And in our urban world, to fear the over-friendly stranger or a person acting strangely is also vital.

On the other hand, being too afraid is a real handicap – children also need to be able to speak to adults, talk up at school and get their needs met, and join in socially. They need to see the world as a basically safe place, if handled properly. We'd like them to be brave enough to try new things – sports, new friends, creativity, and so on.

Fear has two purposes. It focuses you. A snake rearing up in front of you on a bush track soon stops you being dreamy and careless. Fear also energises you. You will run faster and jump logs higher than you thought possible!

What kids need to learn in order to deal with fear is summed up in one word – THINK. We use our minds to sort out our fears. To plan for what we may need to do. When my job involved a lot of flying around the country, I found myself becoming more and more unhappy on planes. They felt unsafe – high up, bumping through clouds, wings flexing and so on. I had to check myself out – that no Australian jetliner had ever crashed, that plane travel is safer than road travel, that all around the world thousands of jets are routinely in the air all the time. And I found this worked. This is exactly the approach I take with kids.

Four basic hints for dealing with fears:

1. BE VERY MATTER OF FACT. Three- and four-year-old children often start to think more about the wide world around them, and come up with lots of concerns – this stage is even known as the 'fearful fours' in some books. Talk it over with them, be patient but casual. Trust their intuition – sometimes their caution about people or places will be well founded. Fear is a kind of radar, which has served the human race well through a dangerous past.

2. TALK FEARS OVER. If a child raises a realistic (if remote) fear, then explain the unlikelihood of it happening, but do figure out an action plan – figuring out with them what they would need to do to feel safe again.

3. IF THEY RAISE AN UNREALISTIC FEAR, TELL THEM SO. Don't search under their bed for monsters, unless you live in the Komodo Islands or somesuch!

4. UNDERLYING FEARS. If they are constantly fearful, use your listening skills to search out if there is something else that is troubling them, which they find hard to tell you. Sometimes one fear is a cover for another that is harder to share.

Because of the different kinds of danger facing children today, especially living in large impersonal cities, a program called

Protective Behaviours Training is being introduced in many schools. Protective Behaviours helps children plan for how and where to get help, if anything at all happens. Sadly one of the most common dangers children face is sexual abuse – usually from someone known to their family.

Protective Behaviours teaches two rules: 'There is nothing so bad that you can't tell someone about it' and 'You have a right to feel safe all the time'. (If only that were true for the whole world!) It skilfully avoids teaching younger children the specifics of sexual abuse – those experiencing it know these all too well, and those who aren't don't really need to. The program does not quiz or identify individual kids in the classroom. It does give strategies for getting support people for each child, so that those who are in (or may encounter) danger know clearly how to get help. The reporting of verifiable sexual abuse has been found to increase markedly in the months after the program is introduced. The incidence of child abuse is also claimed to fall when the program is well publicised, probably because the offending adults realise that being found out is a real risk.

A strength of the program is that it deals largely with everyday dangers – such as arriving home to find the house locked and no-one in; or getting on the wrong bus. It's a brilliant balance between some programs which simply frighten kids but don't inform them, or the alternative – to leave them ignorant and helpless. We learned from Protective Behaviours how to teach our kids safety-thinking skills. If the program isn't in your child's school, ask why not!

In summary, kids need a little fear in their lives to protect them. They don't need overloading with adult fears – it's our job to take care of those. They need teaching how to think through danger situations, and one good way is to plan with them: 'What would you do if …' in response to questions they ask, or dangers you want to prepare them for.

Rackets – when feelings get out of hand

We all have an intuitive sense that there is a difference between a real emotion, and one that is 'put on'. Children often get such a good reaction when they show a particular emotion, that they learn to run out that feeling whenever they want the desired effect. Each set of parents will have their buttons pressed by the feelings they most sympathise with. The child thus learns the emotion 'most likely to succeed'.

Feelings that are 'faked' by a child in this way are called 'racket feelings' (though we're looking for a kinder word).

Anger when put on as a racket is called a *tantrum*.

Sadness when put on as a racket, is called *sulking*.

Fear when put on as a racket is called *shyness*.

These three rackets comprise some of the major challenges to parents of young kids, so let's look at practical approaches to each …

GETTING ON TOP OF TANTRUMS!

Tantrums are learned by accident. A child of eighteen months to two years old is often learning to handle frustration, to wait for things, to take no for an answer. So the first time a tantrum occurs, they are simply swept away with the force of their own rage, and behave in an out-of-control way that neither you or they have ever experienced before. Sometimes this is so sudden that the child is scared too! 'What was THAT!!' – and they will cry afterwards and need reassurance. From here on though, the toddler is aware of

what they are doing, and IS actually in control. 'Well, look at that, I'm screaming at the top of my lungs – now, here goes with the flailing on the ground – a bit of a dribble – that's the way!'

Why would anyone want to behave this way? Partly its just the relief of discharging all that built up frustration. But most of the motivation is the effect on big people! Big people gets really embarrassed, frightened, uptight, and sometimes they give you what you want! Thus tantrums, as an anger racket, can become ingrained.

So here's what to do:

1. END THE PAYOFFS. The very first essential step is to make up your mind. You will never again give a child what they want as a result of them throwing a tantrum. You might have in the past (for the sake of peace) but not any more.

2. HANDLE THE PRACTICALITIES. Do whatever you need to get through a tantrum once it has started. Some people will walk away, and ignore them (which we would find very hard to do), some scruff them and take them to their room or to a waiting car. It's up to you, and the situation. What is more important is future prevention. Which brings us to the next step ...

3. FOLLOW UP. Once the tantrum is over, don't leave it at that. Let the child know expressing anger in this way is just not on. This is the teaching time when both you and your child are calm enough. They are to stay in their room, or stand by the wall, or wait until you both get home from the supermarket, and then

deal with it — say sorry, say what was bugging them in the first place, say what they should have done differently. And maybe (if it's a bad tantrum, or a repeat performance) some practical consequence — removal of a toy, no TV that day, or whatever.

4. PLAN BETTER. Tantrums often indicate that both the parent and child are living under too much stress. If you want an easier life, recognise that certain situations are frustrating for you and the kids. Therefore do what you can do to minimise such times. Can you arrange to do your big shopping trips while your kids are minded? Or train them, through shorter trips, to get used to being with you but not receiving much of your attention. Make arrangements so that at times when you know you will be busy and stressed there is something else for them to do, or someone else to be with them for an hour or two.

So, let's sum up again on this most common of parents' bugbears. Never let a tantrum pay off. If one gets started, either ignore or safely contain the child according to the needs of the situation. After it's over, make the consequences outlast the situation. This is the time to make sure they know what they could do differently another time in order to get what they were wanting. Get in first if you see a child starting to wind up. Catch them off guard! Finally, avoid the most trying circumstances for you and the child if possible.

Tantrums don't need to be a part of childhood at all. Most kids will 'try it on' but if we handle it this stage will quickly pass.

BEAN BAGGING – HOW TO STOP THE SULKS

It's very dramatic! They are sitting in the bean bag, in the middle of the lounge. You can't miss them. They aren't hiding their anguish! They issue loud and heart-rending sighs. Their face would win an Academy Award for special effects. You can't ignore them, so you ask, 'What's the matter???'. The answer is time honoured – 'Nothin'. And that's only round one!

Sulking is aimed at proving something – to get you to show by your efforts that you care. You prove you care by hovering and guessing, 'Is it the food?', 'Was it something someone said?', 'How are things at school?', 'Are you not feeling too good?'. 'Nope, nuh, uh–uh ...'

Eventually they allow you to give them some sort of special treatment, but even then they are not really right – just mollified temporarily, nursing deep existential hurt until the next time! You wonder if you are somehow deeply inadequate as a father or mother.

Enough! Sulking only works if parents feel guilty in the first place, and so the child has learned to exploit this guilt. Perhaps you woke one night in a daze when they were a baby, accidentally took off their clean nappy and put on a dirty one! Or you stuck them with the nappy pin and now they've got post-traumatic stress. Whatever you're feeling guilty about, if it is in the past, forget it – your guilt won't help your kids.

If we give attention and love to a child who is sulking, they learn a simple equation – love comes through being miserable. If you want to be cared for, just collapse yourself and work up a negative attitude, and people will give you free attention. The problem with this is that it becomes a way of life. Sulks make a career of misery!

I encounter lots of kids and adults who sulk. Once upon a time I would have worked hard to win them over, please them, draw them out. I was the 'feel good man' (though on the inside increasingly tired and angry). Now I am much more effective in changing patterns. If a child sulks around me, I let them know 'I care about you. I'd like to help. Think about what you really want. I'll be in the kitchen'. And I leave them. Usually they come along and get more direct, and then I'm happy to help. Sulking is boring when you don't have anyone to sulk at.

Here are five key beliefs for an anti-sulk campaign:

1. Everyone — child or adult — does know what they want. They just need to think about it until they are clear.
2. Children can learn to ask for what they want, directly, in words.
3. People *need* very little — food, shelter, air, affection, exercise.
4. All the rest are *wants*. And you don't always get what you want!
5. Whether you feel happy or unhappy doesn't affect the world one bit. You may as well be happy.

THE MYTH OF SHYNESS

Do you have a shy child in your family? Well, after you've read this, you may want to change that! You see, shyness is a myth. It's a trap that kids get caught in, and don't know how to get out of. And while shyness may be cute in a child, it is a real handicap in later life. For the truth is, shy people miss out.

So how do kids get to be shy, and how can we help them to be more outgoing? Shyness starts by a mixture of accident and conditioning. We are all caught unawares in social situations sometimes, and get tongue-tied. This happens to kids, too. I once saw a clown go up to a toddler at a show, bend down close, presumably to say hello, and the toddler was nearly scared out of their wits! Actor Robin Williams recounts taking a two-year-old to Disneyland, and finding out from the child's perspective that good ol' Mickey looked like an eight-foot RAT!

It's our job as parents to get our kids past this stage. After all, the people you introduce your kids to shouldn't be either dangerous or scary — so there's no need to act as if they are.

Here are the steps:

1. TEACH YOUR CHILDREN HOW TO BE SOCIABLE. This is very simple. When someone speaks to your child, or says hello, and you are around, explain to them that they should:
   - look up at the person who has spoken to them
   - say hello and add the person's name

   You can introduce people, saying 'This is Peter (or Doctor Brown, or whoever), say hello to him, please!'. The child looks up and says 'Hello Peter', and that's it! For kids under four, leave it at that. They should not be the centre of attention for more than a moment or two – or they will be pressured into being little performers. Saying hello and making eye contact is a good start.

2. INSIST THAT THEY DO IT! Three-year-old Angela was considered by her parents to be very shy. They often had guests visiting, and although Angela was boisterous and talkative at other times, she would become coy, hide behind her mother's skirts, and generally be awkward when new people were around. This behaviour was extended to her meetings with other children.

Her parents talked to us, and decided on a course of action. They gave her clear instructions about how to look up and speak when spoken to. When a friend, who had often been before, came to visit, and Angie acted shy instead of saying hello, they told her to go and stand and think until she was ready to get it right. (Stand and think is a technique used by many parents now to help kids think a problem through – an alternative to smacks or yelling.) Angie stood by the wall, but made a fuss, and was taken to her room. (By this time her parents were glad it was an old friend they had, and not some judgemental strangers.) It usually takes effort to break through a pattern the first time. When Angie quietened down, she was brought back to the room. She immediately said 'I'm ready'. (She may be stubborn, but not stupid.) She then came out, easy as pie, and said 'Hello Maggie' to the visitor, and ran off and played happily. Soon afterwards, she approached Maggie easily and showed her a toy and chatted. The problem hardly ever occurred again, and when it did a few secondsto stand and think sorted it out. Angela went from being a shy child to an outgoing one in a matter of days.

The only reason shyness persists in the first place is that some adults give so much attention to it. They think it is cute, lovable and endearing, and make a great show of 'drawing a child out'. The child gets more attention than they ever would for just being straightforward.

The only times when kids should be scared of people are when you are not around, or when there is something amiss, eg. an adult who is actually dangerous, drunk, or known or intuited by the child to be a sexual danger. These people should not be around your children in the first place. Watch out for extreme reactions in your kids, and as soon as possible find out the reason.

Outgoingness is really just a matter of getting started with people, being friendly and making a move – and then things flow easily. By teaching your child to say hello, to make eye contact and introduce themselves, they will make friends, enjoy people and their skills will grow. They will have a more successful life in all sorts of ways – socially, at school and in their career. Well worth sorting out early on.

Some children and adults are naturally more quiet and self-contained. Don't force your child to be an extrovert – just make sure they can be sociable when the need arises.

5

The assertive parent

Firmness. Do it – now.

In my early work with families, I was always having my eyes opened in one way or another. One of the first big surprises was to discover that some of the most stable and happy children were being brought up by incredibly firm (to my way of thinking) parents. The secret seemed to be that these parents were hard but reliable – so consistent that their children knew exactly what the rules were and how to stay out of trouble. Because of this, they received punishment very rarely.

Most importantly, these children knew that they were loved and valued unconditionally. Rejection was never a possibility. These kids would have sometimes been afraid, but never terrified and never made to feel abandoned. In brief, there were strong rules plus positive affection. If there had been one without the other I don't think it would have succeeded.

In contrast to these firm-but-fair families, I saw far more children who had lots of 'freedom', got away with dreadful misbehaviour but were still miserable. Clearly, these children were looking for someone to put the brakes on them, and their parents misunderstood the signals. They thought the children wanted more room and more freedom, but the opposite was true.

Children's need for limits is one of the secrets that parents need to know about. When social workers place a child in a foster home, after that child's own home has disintegrated, they have learned to warn the foster parents:

'This child may settle in easily but, more probably, he will play up a great deal in the first three months to test out you and your family unit – to see if it is strong enough to hold him. He will want to know if your marriage, your mental health, your affection and your discipline are strong enough. *Then* he can relax and begin to grow again.

In short, he wants to know that this family will not break like the old one, and will test it to see!'

Fostering is the extreme example. But all children are the same: they need to know that someone is going to stop them.

We know from research that there are three main styles of parental response to children's playing up: aggressive, passive and assertive. Aggressive parents use attack, either in words or action, to put their children down. Passive parents allow children to 'walk over' them and only regain control when it's 'the last straw' – and then by unexpected outbursts. Assertive parents are quite different. Let me explain the three to you in more detail.

The aggressive parent

Aggressive parents are angry with their children nearly all the time. Usually their anger is not a result of the child's behaviour at all. They may perhaps be resenting their marriage, their jobs, the human race, or the fact that they're parents and don't want to be (which is no fault of the children). They let out this tension by putting the children down.

Some children deal with this in a very interesting way. They realise that this is a kind of love, reasoning thus: 'At least they're interested enough to yell at me, and they yell loudly so they must care a lot!'. The child may even yell back (to return the love), and soon parents and children are relating by fighting – kind of a 'Bratty Bunch'! Whole families can join in. What to an outsider looks like a dangerous free-for-all is actually a kind of intimacy which all the participants would miss if it weren't going on!

Other children, sensing that parental put-downs are really destructive in intent, become withdrawn and disturbed.

As far as obedience is concerned, aggressive parents do get results, based on fear. However, they also get rebellion: many a bullying parent has one day faced a teenager big enough to hit back. Aggressive parents end up with children who are either frightened and intimidated or rebellious and defiant – or a mixture of both!

The passive parent

Passive parents are everywhere!

I once interviewed a young mother who complained about her child's disobedience. This was quite a common complaint but there were one or two unusual things that caught my notice. Most parents bring the child with them to see me. In fact, many would like to drop them off, saying, 'Here, you fix her!'. This mother had not brought the child 'for fear of upsetting her (and had not told her husband either).

As we talked, she poured out details of the child's behaviour, obviously relieving herself of enormous worry and tension by putting it into words. She seemed so keen to unburden herself that it was a good half hour before I needed to speak. I asked how she dealt with disobedience and she replied that she was very firm but the child simply did not obey. I asked her to bring the child next time and show me.

The child was very cooperative and lived up to our expectations. After a few minutes 'casing the joint', she set about dismantling my telephone and curtains. I asked the mother to show me how she would stop the child. She immediately dropped her voice and murmured in soft, cautious tones, 'Melissa darling, how about stopping that?'.

Naturally, there was no change. 'Please, love, come here, there's a good girl.'

I liked this lady: she was an involved parent and wanted to do what was best for her child. However, her idea of firmness and mine were very different.

Some 'assertiveness training' was tried, and some help to trace and change the causes of her timidity: Melissa soon ceased to be the power in the family!

Good behaviour in children is required not as a whim of parents but to make practical living easier. Unlike parents of the Victorian era, we do not need pointless obedience, such as brushing one's hair before sitting down for tea or eating one's food in alphabetical order! We ask kids to cooperate so as to make life go more smoothly: 'Put on your old clothes before you go out and play', 'Get that cat out of the fridge!'

Therefore, when a child does not cooperate, the parents find their life inconvenienced. Soft parents soon find they are being given the runaround. However much they want to give in and not inhibit little Sebastian's creativity, these parents find they are very angry and tired of the troubles this causes, and attempt to restore order. It may be after an hour of disobedience or a long week of repeated trouble but, whenever it happens, the parents' patience suddenly runs out. They suddenly lash out and discipline the child in a way, and with a feeling, that they and the child know is somewhat out of control.

It will come as no surprise to you that parents who injure children are very often shy, timid parents who finally blow their stack. If you ever feel that you are a danger to your child's safety or your own when you 'blow up', then be sure to read Chapter 8 of this book to find out more about self-care.

As I write this, I'm feeling a lot of concern that you, the reader, may be feeling bad, recognising yourself in some of the above. If you have this pattern in your relationship with your child (back down, back down, back down, blow up) then you need to know a couple of things.

- About a third of parents experience this pattern, especially when they have young children, and are just beginning to gain experience in parenting.
- It is not a big problem, just a misdirection of your energies and can be remedied.

So aggressive and passive parenting don't work – what's left? Finally (with a trumpet fanfare!) we announce the ASSERTIVE PARENT.

The assertive parent

Assertive parents are clear, firm, determined and, on the inside, fairly confident and relaxed. Their children learn that what Mum or Dad says goes but, at the same time, that they will not be treated with put-downs or humiliation.

Assertiveness is not something you see every day and so you may not have a lot of examples to copy from. If your parents were aggressive, then it may be particularly hard for you to be assertive. The important thing is to see assertiveness as a skill, not something that you are born with. This means that you may take time to learn it. There's still hope!

The first part of assertiveness is on the inside of you, in your attitudes. Circle which is closer to describing you.

'Mush' parents devalue themselves	'Firm' parents decide they matter too
• I come last in the family.	• I'm as important as the rest of the family.
• I have to keep the kids happy all the time or I'm a bad parent.	• The children are important, but they have to fit in with others, too.
• I mustn't frustrate their natural creativity.	• Frustration is part of growing up: the kids can't always get their way.
• I'm nobody, really, but my kids might be someone someday.	• I need to be happy and healthy to be a good parent – I have to do things for myself, too.
• My spouse matters but not as much as the kids.	• My partner and our marriage are very important. The kids come an equal first.
• Life is such a struggle.	• Life is challenging but fun.
• I just want to keep the peace: I give in to the kids for the sake of some peace and quiet. Pity it doesn't last long.	• Life is easier if kids learn to behave well. As an adult I am the one in charge.

The second part of assertiveness lies in action: what you actually do. Here is how to get good behaviour from a child who is used to disobeying or delaying.

1. **Be clear in your own mind.** What you're asking of your child is not a request, its not open to debate: it's a demand which you have a right to make, and the child will benefit from learning to carry it out.

2. **Make good contact.** Stop what you are doing, go up close to the child and get him to look at you. Don't give the instruction until he looks at you.

3. **Be clear.** Say, 'I want you to . . . now. Do you understand?'. Make sure you get a 'yes' or 'no' answer.

4. **If they do not obey repeat what you want from them.** Do not discuss, reason, get angry or scared. Breathe slowly and deeply so that you become calmer. What you are signalling to the child is that you are willing to persist on this one and not even get upset about it. This is the key step, and what matters most is what you don't do. You don't enter into debate or argument, you don't get heated, you simply repeat the demand to the child.

5. **Stay close** if there is any chance that the child will not carry out the task fully. When the task is completed (say, putting away toys) then don't make much of this either. Simply say, 'Good,' and smile briefly!

This sequence is a *retraining procedure*. It may well be time-consuming the first couple of times, so that you'll think, 'Boy, it's easier for me to put the toys away!'. But the time invested here will be repaid a thousandfold.

The trick is simply to persist. When the child discovers that you do not give up, give an entertaining minor nervous breakdown, or get sidetracked then he simply gives in.

You will find that you soon develop a tone of voice and a posture that says 'I mean business' to your child. It's completely different from the voice that you use to discuss, tease, praise or play with your child. The child will recognise it as the voice that means 'Do it now!'. And they do! It's a great feeling!

Once they've cottoned on to assertive parenting, it's amazing to look back at how you used to make things hard for yourself. For example, here is the great Australian bedtime drama. Names have been changed to protect the innocent!

It's right on Cheryl's bedtime.

Mum	Child (to herself)
It's nearly bedtime, Cheryl. Better start packing up!	*She said 'nearly' – that means 'not yet'.*
Are you packing up your toys?	*Some chance!*
You know how tired you get in the mornings, dear . . .	*Mum's using reasoning with me – that means she's scared of me. Anyhow, morning is years away still.*
Come on, Cheryl, you don't want to cause another fuss, do you?	*Yep.*
Look, I'll help you put the dolls away.	*Goody! Mummy's gonna play with me!*
Hey, put those toys back. I just packed them away.	*Catch me!*
Cheryl, do you want me to get really cross?	*Yes! It's exciting.*
You're a naughty, naughty child.	*I suppose I am. I don't know why, but I really enjoy these fights. They really get Mum involved.*

The child's answers are, of course, unspoken. If Mum heard them she might not have been so willing to play along. The same sequence occurs in many situations. The main steps are:

- the parents fear conflict: they sound reluctant and doubtful when they first 'ask' the child to cooperate;
- they use reasoning and argument, not seeing that this is being used by the child to 'buy time';
- they give a lot of attention to struggling with the child, who enjoys the control and interest of having a big person on a string;
- the parents become fed up and crack down with more emotion and putdowns than they really wanted to use.

It's painful, especially if it happens every day. Thank goodness there's a way out.

One way to be angry and relaxed at the same time — pretend!

One day when I was at school, our science teacher was called out of the room. Soon we had out the squeeze bottles of distilled water and were re-enacting the gunfight at the OK Corral from behind the benches.

Although normally a timid child, I had got myself out to the front of the lab and was blazing away at the others, when suddenly their faces changed and they went still. A roar came from behind me and the teacher was back amongst us in a fury!

I was back in my desk almost by magic and didn't dare to even look up from my book. When I did, an amazing thing met my eye. The teacher was looking out over the silent class, grinning from ear to ear. I realised that he had been *acting* angry and was amused by the instant results he had achieved as a result.

This was new to me. I knew adults who got angry and went out of control, and others who got scared of their own anger, so that it came out all uneven. I decided that I liked this new kind better but that I'd stay in my seat in future.

We've explained discipline methods in more detail in *More Secrets of Happy Children*. If you're having serious problems – drugs, crime, etc. – a superb book called *Tough Love* gives very practical help plus parent support networks (see *References* on p. 136).

The whole human race has been working out the discipline question for the last 30 or 40 years, so you're not alone. Until this century, children weren't much of a problem: two-thirds of them died; the remainder were seen as of little consequence unless they got to their teens and then they were classed as adults. Violence was the standard means of control. These were the days when seven-year-olds were sent down unventilated mines or stood at factory machines for ten-hour days. Childhood is looking up.

In the 50s and 60s came the great era of letting children be special. Like all new movements, the pendulum swung a little too far, so that youngsters found themselves with the troublesome burden of being the most important person in the whole family. Needless to say, this wasn't very good for them either. Finally, the pendulum is settling in the middle. We are learning to give both soft love and tough love, and our kids are starting to calm down.

So, that's the story on assertive parenting. It starts with the decision that you as a parent have rights, and that your child *needs* your control (even though he or she may not agree). It ends with a much quieter life for everyone, and a lot more time for fun.

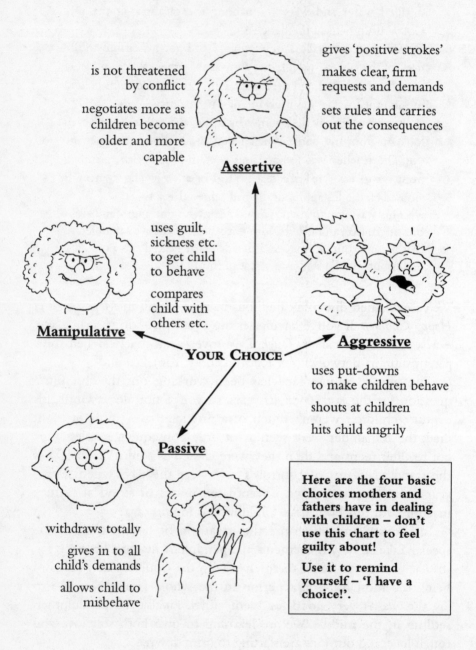

gives 'positive strokes'

makes clear, firm requests and demands

sets rules and carries out the consequences

is not threatened by conflict

negotiates more as children become older and more capable

Assertive

uses guilt, sickness etc. to get child to behave

compares child with others etc.

Manipulative

YOUR CHOICE

Aggressive

uses put-downs to make children behave

shouts at children

hits child angrily

Passive

withdraws totally

gives in to all child's demands

allows child to misbehave

Here are the four basic choices mothers and fathers have in dealing with children – don't use this chart to feel guilty about!

Use it to remind yourself – 'I have a choice!'.

FATHERING — BACKING UP YOUR PARTNER

Many things in life are more easily done with someone else as backup, and one of those things is raising kids.

There's no doubt that handling kids takes determination, grit and purpose in order to get them back in line. Nothing feels better at these times than knowing you have the backup of your spouse.

Most people got a little shy of backup for a time, because they wanted to avoid the OLD WAY of doing things. What was the OLD WAY? It can be summed up in one sentence — 'Wait till your father gets home!'. This was not a fun arrangement — Mum alone and overwhelmed, drops the disciplinary role onto Dad, who, when he gets home just wants to relax, but ends up being the bad guy to the kids, who then get away with murder over Mum when he's gone again, and so on.

Backup is important, but it has to be done properly. There is one simple rule: when you back someone up, you don't need to take over.

Relationships are simpler if people deal with each other directly. Whenever communication becomes three-handed, it gets confused. Here is an example of how to stay straight …

Peter, aged thirteen, is hassling with Marjorie, his Mum, about putting out dirty clothes to be washed. He gets louder and begins to swear, and is talking too aggressively. His father overhears this, and walks in. He tells Peter 'Hey! You need to use a normal voice and sort this out with your mother now'. He catches Peter's eye. 'Right?' 'Mmm.' Dad then walks off, but stays within earshot. Peter then has to continue and solve the problem about the clothes.

The principle is this — a child who is dealing with their mother over something has to complete that process with Mum. Where a father comes in is to ensure that the child is respectful and gets on with it. In this way everything is kept simple.

The need for backup can occur when dealing with both girls and boys. However, boys especially seem at certain ages to go in for concerted limit testing — and it's handy to have Dad to 'bring on the cavalry'. But backing up should be available both ways. Both parents have to strike a balance of firmness and kindness too. You can't 'make up for' another parent's hardness or softness — each has to be a rounded person to the child.

Another OLD WAY that seems to have been incredibly common 30 years ago was the hard parent/soft parent combination – when one parent tried to make up for the other's harshness. Dad sends you to bed with no dinner, but Mum sneaks in with scones and jam! This doesn't work too well, since the child doesn't experience either parent being balanced.

Like everything else in parenting, you'll find a way that suits you. You'll know you're getting it right when your child says 'That's not fair! You're both against me!' – but doesn't seem too put out about it most of the time!

KIDS AND HOUSEWORK — HOW TO TEACH RESPONSIBILITY

Here is a neat way to reduce the housework you have to do, and help your kids get ready for adult life — all at the same time!

In Australia kids have it very easy. We are often amazed to hear of young adults — in their twenties — living at home, being cooked for and having their laundry done by their ageing parents! A lot of Aussie kids don't grow up (that is, don't take responsibility for their own care and feeding) until they are in their early twenties. This is especially true of young men. Perhaps you are married to one!

All around the world, from Nepal to New Guinea to Nicaragua, it's normal for young children to have responsibilities. They are usually under watchful adult care (not neglected like many affluent western children) but they have a daily round of chores which they carry out quite cheerfully and with obvious pride. There is also time for play, of course. The result of this working childhood is that in almost every other culture of the world, childhood flows smoothly and easily into adult life. How did we ever get the idea that childhood is a 'waiting room' before real life begins?

Can we do a better job of helping our kids get ready for self-sufficiency in adulthood? Of course — and one way is by giving them work to do. You can start very early, from two years, when kids can have a small daily task, like putting out the cutlery for dinner.

The tasks increase month by month. Choose tasks which are regular and easy, involving self-care, and some which contribute to the overall family welfare. By four they could set the table, as well as take their dishes to the sink. As they get older you will easily be able to think of tasks which you can add on. Remind them, and follow up on them, and in time simply expect them to remember. Give praise and be proud of them, but don't go overboard — this is no big deal, just what is expected.

Much is made these days of self-esteem and the importance of praising and valuing kids and their efforts. It's more important to remember that real self-esteem comes from contributing. Without knowing their place, and having a contribution, kids may get a kind of 'Young Talent' self-image — a ballooned idea of themselves which the big world away from a doting Mum and Dad will be sure to deflate.

This casual, graduated approach makes later stages much easier. Teenagers who have been helping out for as long as they can remember will not have the resistance to pulling their weight – it will simply be routine. You're aiming for a young person who by the age of eighteen is doing as much work around the house as either parent. Cooking at least one family meal per week, being responsible for some other area of family care. If sharing tasks between children, give them a mixture of the ones they like, and enjoy, but also a proportion that are less pleasant. Again you are aiming to be realistic – just as in adult life.

What about study? Some adjustment may have to be made at times of exam pressure. But by and large, study and homework are simply their 'day jobs', and shouldn't prevent them from making a contribution at home.

Remember, you are aiming for competence in all the basic areas of life – cooking, cleaning, laundry, care of animals, budgeting, time-management, as well as negotiation and team-work! When your youngsters leave home, they'll do so fully equipped to look after themselves. In fact they'll probably leave sooner to escape all the work!

6
Family shape

Dad? Who's Dad?

What comes into your mind when you hear the word, 'family'? Older people would conjure up a gathering of 30 or 40 people – aunts, uncles, cousins and others. Relatives who very likely lived in the same district and got together many times a year, if not weekly for Sunday dinner.

What we call families today are not families at all. We haven't had real families since the car was invented, and we became dispersed. The 'two-parent, three kids and golden labrador' family is only a piece of family – and that's why it doesn't work very well.

What's more, the picture above is changing, too. The average Australian family is now often either a single-parent family, or a recombined family with only one of the child's parents and a new Dad or Mum, probably with their kids. This isn't necessarily a bad thing, but it is making life very different.

How does all this affect your children? Well, we have discovered that the shape of your family is very important, and you can alter its shape to make it a good place to be.

So read on!

Here then is the Steve Biddulph plan for government policy-making on families!

Let's use an example. Some people blamed all social ills on family breakdown:

'Where are you orf to, young Merv?'

'Just off with the guys to steal a car, Mum!'

'Well, don't be late home!'

Superficially, this is true, but what caused the families to break down? Have you ever seen the places where street gangs grow up? Or living conditions in Belfast or Soweto?

Income levels are important to start with. Below certain standards of 'liveability', no one can raise happy children. Above a certain point, though, the need changes from material to human resources. Education, the development of community, ways to belong and participate and work together with others, emerge as the strongest needs for healthy family life.

This, in dollar terms, is very cheap. A friend of mine organises self-help groups for people who've had breakdowns. If he keeps two people per year out of hospital, he pays for his own salary. In fact, he achieves much more than that.

For thousands of years people lived in villages or small towns.

When modern cities began to appear, about 200 years ago, people still lived pretty much in the same neighbourhood as all their relatives. So the family unit looked something like the illustration on the following page.

As you can see, it's quite a gathering of people. And although times were hard, with people dying in wars and a lot of deaths in childbirth or infancy, this extended family unit was very supportive. For example:

> Mavis (who stayed single) loves kids, and so often has little Jenny to stay with her. This is good for Doris, with the three boys. Doris is often unwell and Mavis cooks and helps clean once or twice a week.
>
> Enid's husband, Len, died in the war. Angus was born in 1920, which could have caused a few problems, considering the war ended in 1918, but, since Enid moved in with Wilf and Naomi, no one outside the family needed to know!
>
> Grandpa is a little over the hill and keeps waking up thinking the Boers are coming but, luckily, Branston, the youngest son, is staying on at home and looking after the farm.
>
> Wilfred doesn't like children and is often away, but Arthur likes children and so takes the boys fishing, playing cricket, and so on – so they don't miss out too badly.

The 24 people in this hypothetical family don't actually live together (there are six households in all) but it would be a rare week that they didn't all see each other at some time or other. The family unit was able to withstand wars, illnesses, deaths, Enid's 'flying Scotsman' and various failings and foibles; and everyone belonged and was cared for.

It was a hard time, but there was less uncertainty. For parents, this had definite advantages. Right was right and wrong was wrong. If you weren't everything your children needed, there were others to step in. You were never alone – there was plenty of advice, help and example. You got lots of practice with other people's children and your younger brothers and sisters before you started on your own. You could even choose not to have kids at all and still not be too lonely.

There were lots of restrictions and demands, too, and not many of us would go back, even if we could, to that kind of extended family. But the good things that were there for parents – could we ever get those back? I think so, and would like to tell you how.

THE EXTENDED FAMILY OF YESTERYEAR

Grandma's sisters ———————————▶ Grandma
Jane and Doreen   (had 9 kids
(Jane's husband Roy dec.)   3 died in birth
                                  or infancy)

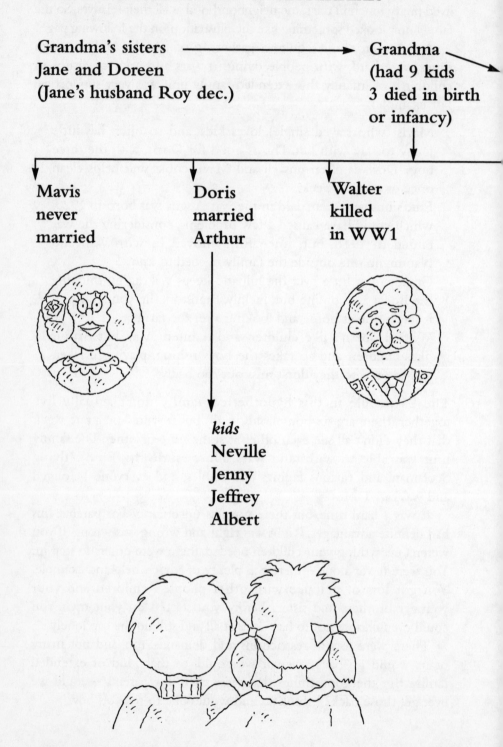

Mavis
never
married

Doris
married
Arthur

Walter
killed
in WW1

kids
Neville
Jenny
Jeffrey
Albert

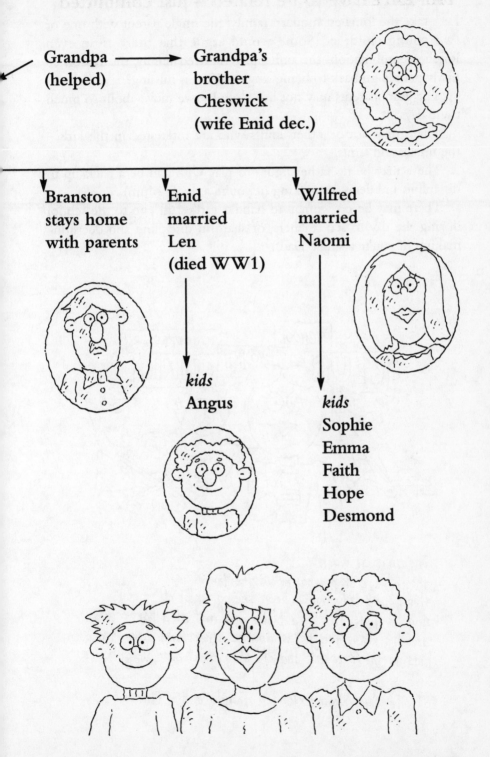

Grandpa
(helped) → Grandpa's
brother
Cheswick
(wife Enid dec.)

Branston
stays home
with parents

Enid
married
Len
(died WW1)

kids
Angus

Wilfred
married
Naomi

kids
Sophie
Emma
Faith
Hope
Desmond

You don't have to be related – just committed

Let's take the loneliest modern family: the single parent with one or two young children. (Some would argue that there is an even lonelier combination: the unhappily married family, the reason so many people go back to being single.) What is missing?

The grandparents may not live close by: we move about so much these days.

There may not be other adults who are interested in the kids – the uncles and aunts.

There may be no father figure to play with and be a back-up in discipline and decision-making (if you're a single Mum).

There may be no woman to handle 'girl's stuff', go to the school during the day to see teachers, or share in discipline and decision-making (if you're a single Dad).

The girls at work
the teenage chap who mows the lawn
this young lady you've been seeing a lot of,
and her kids. This nice bloke you met at a barbecue
and his kids, the fellas up the street who take the
kids to the cricket, the old lady, next door neighbours

"The Australian Extended Family of the Future!"

There may not be other kids to play with or safe places outside the house or flat for the kids to go.

When really hard things happen there's no-one to talk to that you can really trust or who will help you materially, just because you're 'family'.

But the fact that all of these things are not available doesn't mean that they may not be found. For instance, some old people really like kids. Might it be possible to find some 'grandpersons' who live nearby, who could become part of your family? (You paint their ceiling, they mind your kids!)

There are other single parents, or not-single parents, dying of loneliness very close to you. Do you think people really go to Tupperware parties to buy plastic bowls? They go for something to do, and someone to talk to. Other parents are dying to talk to you.

You can find out about groups that have been started in the community. Playgroups are really just like Sunday afternoon at Grandma's place, where kids can play and parents can talk and join in. Courses run by adult education centres are good meeting places and very friendly. Schools, kinder, infant health centres, environment groups, gym, churches – choose whatever suits your style.

It's very hard work, and if you move you have to start all over again. Nonetheless, you can actually make yourself an extended family if not for your own sake, then for your children's.

There's another part of family shape that is very important, even if your family is the official two adults and two-and-a-bit kids.

When you started out as a couple it was simple. There were just the two of you, and you probably had a good time.

Then, when kids were added in, it might have started to get complicated. Many families find themselves caught in one of these 'shapes':

You've probably experienced all three at some time. And with more kids, the combinations can get even tougher:

These are natural alignments for the family from time to time, but they are bad news if they become the normal shape of your family.

What we have found in hundreds of families seeking help is that *the closeness of the parent-couple is very important.* Kids seem to grow up most easily and happily when Mum and Dad are affectionate and interested in each other – to such a degree that the children could not come between them, even if they tried (which they do!).

One expert became famous for saying that the best sex education in the world was for Dad to give Mum a pinch as he walked past her in the kitchen, and for Mum to obviously enjoy it! All the rest, he said, was just so much plumbing! In the interests of non-sexism, I'm sure it would be just as good the other way around (Mum pinching Dad!).

Kids actually seem to gain reassurance from the fact that parents spend time together and they are not allowed to interrupt. If you haven't been in the habit of doing this (so that the kids have first call on you even when you are talking to your partner) – then you should set about to break the pattern.

Problems seem to arise whenever:

- a parent frequently sides with a child against the other parent;
- a parent seeks affection and approval from a child, in preference to, or instead of, his or her spouse;
- a child is forced into a parent role too often, for example, having to care for other children or being part of decisions that are really parents' decisions.

I was furious once to hear a well-meaning relative tell a nine-year-old boy, whose father had just died, that he would have to 'be a man now and take care of your mother'. Kids should be kids!

Every person is different and no advice can be completely right. All I can do is give you the general rules that we have found, and which may apply to you and your children.

- In a single-parent family, kids are happier when their parent has a close, affectionate relationship with another adult. Whether it is their natural parent or not, or whether the other adult is the opposite sex or not, doesn't matter greatly; what matters is that their parent is happily supported by at least one special 'other' adult.
- Children suffer if conflict is ongoing, but they also suffer in marriage breakups. The research is very clear on this. Couples owe it to themselves to get good counselling and help to work on their difficulties. All marriages have tough patches – don't panic. Unless your partner is violent, addicted, chronically dishonest, or totally refuses to communicate, your chances of improving things are very good. But it takes work.

A couple recently appeared in the Family Court to obtain a divorce. The man was ninety-one and his wife eighty-six.

The judge asked why they were getting divorced after all these years. They replied, as many couples before had, 'We can't stand each other!'.

'But why did you stay together all these years?' asked the Judge in dismay.

'Because,' said the couple, 'we wanted to wait until the children had died'.

BUT WHAT IF YOU'RE A SINGLE MUM?

Single parenthood has both advantages and disadvantages. The advantages are that you don't have to put up with differing standards, conflicts between parents, and so on. You're the boss! Separated mothers have often told us that life is a lot smoother. On the other hand, many things, like discipline, are harder to do by yourself. Let's look at this.

Sometimes as kids are growing up, it's necessary to 'lean on' them with a lot of strength and persistence. You can see the need to bring them into line, for your sake and theirs, but it just gets tiring. At certain ages boys especially are hard for single mothers to manage. It seems to be a biological need for some boy children to experience strong conflict, and be firmly and frequently controlled until they learn to temper their strength and rebellion and so get along with other people. Put simply, they actually seem to want a fight, and only relax and let up when you give it to them. At times like these, a father would come in handy.

It seems like fathering, and mothering, are two different kinds of input, both of which kids need, to grow up well. If need be a mother *can* provide fathering, and a man can provide mothering. The lesson of the feminist era is clear – women and men are not so different. A woman *can* do anything a man can do, and vice versa (with some obvious biological exceptions!). The difference is, though, that a man will often find it easier, less against the grain, to be tough on kids.

A mother raising kids alone can muster this hardness, but it will take a lot of energy, because it draws on the male liking for combativeness, which she will not find so readily available. A single mother will need to practise and acquire toughness, and at the same time not lose her compassion and peace-making skills.

Lots of single parents have told us that once they know this, it makes things less mystifying and overwhelming – they just learn to 'change gear'.

COUPLE TIME! THE TEN MINUTES THAT CAN SAVE YOUR MARRIAGE

Would you like to turn the worst time of the day into the best time? Would you like to have romance, warmth, friendship and relaxation in your life? Then try the following ritual. Taken daily – or as needed – you can make evenings go well, and stay happily married. No kidding!

When you and/or your partner arrive home in the evening, you may have got into the habit of putting off relaxation until things were over with – meals, housework, kids, etc. This may work fine when the kids are little and in bed by seven. But not for long – as they get older, you wait longer to be together again.

In the old days, husbands and wives were together more of the time, and got into a rhythm together. The widely differing tempo of our workdays apart means that when we come back together in the family home, we're spinning like tops at different speeds. So it's hard to feel connected. In fact many couples positively clash all night, only starting to synchronise late in the evening, if they have any energy or motivation left!!

Therefore, we need to make sure that we DO get synchronised as soon as we can. The way to do this is as follows:

1. MEET! As soon as you are both home, sit down, and take a few minutes out together. And while you're doing this …
2. EAT! Have some convenient but substantial snack food – salami, nuts, cheese, fruit, fruitcake, something with body in it to fill the hungry gap and give some instant energy. Next step is …
3. KIDS TO ONE SIDE! Children, who are often the only ones who do score any time and attention around teatime, have to stay out of the way. If they can do this in the room, fine – if not, send them out of the room. Their turn will come. Be tough on this one! It's only ten minutes.
4. DRINK. If you drink alcohol at all, make this the time for it. A single wine, beer or sherry, together with the snacks, will help you rapidly slip out of the day's tensions and let your body know this is winding down time.
5. TALK only if you want to. If you do, be sure to talk about good things. Avoid completely the old competition couples play – called 'Who Had the Worst Day?'. Either talk positively, or sit quietly and enjoy just being there.

Soon you'll be settled enough to want to get on with the evening's activities — you can cook a more leisurely meal, since you are no longer desperately hungry, or be with the kids if you are the one who has been absent all day. You'll find that everything flows better because your whole rhythm — even down to your heartbeat — is more synchronised with your partner's.

This daily ritual is so simple, and yet it's effect is profound. It saves marriages. It's as simple as that. Give it a go!

7
Ages and stages
Do you mean this is normal?

Kids *do* change as they grow. What's right to say to a three-year-old could be wrong to say to a seven-year-old, and different again from what you would tell, or require of, a teenager. An idea of stages helps you to know what should be going on at a particular age, and how best to react.

The stages explained in this chapter are adapted from a book called *Self Esteem: A Family Affair*, by Jean Illsley-Clarke (see *References*, p. 136, for details). I've discussed them with thousands of parents and the most frequent response has been 'Aaaaahhh! That's exactly right!' and, sometimes, 'If only we'd known!'.

The stages of child development

0–6 months:	Can I trust these people?
6–18 months:	Explore!
18 months–3 years:	Learning to think.
3–6 years:	Other people.
6–12 years:	I did it my way!
12–18 years:	Getting ready to leave.

Let's look at them in more detail.

Can I trust these people? 0–6 months

The human baby arrives like a being from another planet. Its first thoughts and feelings are pretty blurry, but they are very much to do with:

'Am I safe?'

'Who's gonna feed me?'

'What happened to my waterbed?'

'Those people look nice. How can I keep them around?'

'What's that yucky feeling I'm sitting in?'

It is no use making demands of the new baby, or criticising it, since it is still just 'taking it all in'. It needs you to guess its needs (to be changed, fed, cuddled, burped, carried around) since it has no way of telling you what it wants.

It's important that you don't ignore its cries for help, since it will learn to become passive and depressed if ignored for long. It's equally important to let it *start* to cry heartily for a moment or two, so that it learns that it can *do something* to get its needs met, that its cries will bring help. A child who is always fed *before* it says it's hungry may have trouble knowing what it wants later in life.

Massaging and cuddling the baby, making noises to it, looking at its face and smiling, all make for a happier, brighter child who subsequently sleeps, feeds and learns more easily. Massage has been found to cure constipated babies with amazing speed! (Stand well clear!)

Notice how babies from many of the wiser cultures are carried around in slings and carrybags? One Balinese tradition is the first 'setting down to earth' of a new baby – it does not take place until the child is six months old. Before this it is never out of somebody's arms! We would find this rather unmanageable but it's worth some thought.

Explore the world! 6–18 months

This is the time when, at no charge to you, the child begins to educate himself! He moves out into the big, beautiful world, tasting, grabbing, pushing, carrying, pulling, eating everything in sight.

You can save yourself enormous amounts of energy by creating a *safe, child-proof* zone in your house, so that you don't need to be always saying '*don't*'. Put the stereo up high somewhere, postpone the new wallpaper and your child will be free to wander in peace (yours).

THE EXPLORING STAGE GOES WRONG

In the mid–1970s, I was a very inexperienced psychology graduate, who knew more about rats than about children.

I began work as a School Guidance Officer. My role, according to my superiors, was to take children who, teachers felt, were stupid. I was to administer quaint little tests and then tell the teachers how stupid these children were. This was supposed to be helpful.

I don't really blame my superiors for devising this role. Being responsible for the psychological well-being of 3000 children in nine schools was daunting, and the little tests gave one something concrete to do.

I decided to do something more helpful than just IQ tests. I recruited and trained mothers to coach kids who had fallen behind in reading. I gave talks to teachers about self-esteem. I listened patiently to harassed parents. One day, I went on a home visit to the mother of a boy who was acting up at school . . . The home was out in the country and looked rather run down.

I took off my tie before going in. I talked rather awkwardly with the boy's Mum: she looked very old and tired. On the worn, dusty lino in the kitchen where we talked, a toddler sat looking dully up at us. There was not a Lego block or Dinky Toy in sight. From time to time the child tugged open a cupboard and pulled at the utensils inside. The mother would stand up, rebuke the child, slam the cupboard door and continue talking.

As I drove home, I felt angry and helpless. That Mum's idea of a good toddler was a silent, still toddler. I knew that – without toys to play with and without encouragement to play, or look at books or hear stories – that child, too, would be on the Guidance Officer's list before many years had elapsed: 'suspected mentally deficient'.

Children at this age need to be free of demands to perform, such as sitting up primly, being cute, or being toilet trained (the sphincter muscles that control your child's 'outlets' are not yet sufficiently developed for full control).

Physically, toddlers can be tiring, so this is a good age for you to start getting breaks of a few hours yourself, to rest and do your exploring!

Learning to think – 18 months–3 years

Now the child is starting to use reasoning. It's a good time to give simple explanations for things: 'The kitten gets scared when you squeeze her. I'll show you how to stroke her gently'.

Your child is also using anger and learning to say, 'No, I don't want to,' 'I don't care'. This is the age called by some people 'the terrible twos'. Parents will need to set clear limits.

The child will test these. The parents must remain firm . . . and firm . . . and firm.

Work out ahead of time what is really important and what doesn't matter, to save energy. The child will sometimes want to be independent and then switch back to being very dependent again, especially if a new baby arrives on the scene. This is natural, and the child will soon 'grow up' again if its needs are met.

Other people – 3–6 years

This is the age when children clearly move from playing *alongside* other children to playing *with* other children. It helps if there are other children to learn with. It's also the time of endless questions: when? why? how? what if? why not? and why again?

When they're chattering your ears off, think of this as language development time, and count the money you're saving in remedial tuition and expensive school fees later in life!

Teasing or ridicule by parents, never a good idea, are particularly unhelpful at this age, when the child is learning how to be one of the human race and may easily withdraw.

For robbery with violence. ten years!

But your honour— it's just a stage I'm going through!

Fantasy and reality need to be clearly separated: both are okay, but you need to know the difference.

> 'I'm a monster!'
> 'You're good at *pretending* to be a monster!'
> Growl! Giggle!

Clear requests for appropriate behaviour can be made and are best phrased specifically and positively: 'Pick up your cars now' rather than 'Don't be untidy'.

Vera is the sort of parent who makes you feel like being a little kid. Are you imagining it, or does she actually smell like homemade scones? She's also quick-minded and humorous, and able to put a young psychologist in his place. I decide it's better in this workshop to learn from her than try to teach her, and sure enough I do. Vera recounts how her eight-year-old, Dale, had developed, ever so gradually, a temper that had become a problem to him and to other people. After one particular blow-up of Dale's, Vera had given the matter some careful thought, and then set about a profound and original cure.

She took down an old dusty album of family photos (never before seen by the children) and she and Dale looked through them. Vera pointed out the various family patriarchs, Grandfather Les when he was a boy, Great Uncle Alf, cousin Derek, where they had lived and what they had done. Dale looked with fascination at the weathered faces and ancient clothing styles, while Vera provided the narrative: 'Alf was a good bloke, but very stubborn; Grandfather had quite a temper when he was a boy, so they say'. There was a pause as Dale wondered where this was leading. Vera just turned the pages. 'What happened with his temper, Mum?' 'Oh, he just grew out of it, I suppose. Look, here's his cricket team ...'

Soon the other children came in, and Vera left them with the photos, and went to get the tea. Dale, of course, though he could be firm at times, never lost his temper again. He just grew out of it, I suppose.

I did it my way! 6–12 years

What makes it possible for a six- to twelve-year-old to navigate the world of school, friends, and life generally, is his or her knowledge of the way things work and the 'rules of life'. These rules can be anything from 'If I share my toys with her she'll be my friend' to 'If I don't take my raincoat I'll get wet, and might get a cold and miss out on going ice skating'.

Parents will help by being firm on those rules that are important, but negotiating and compromising on those that are negotiable. The child thus learns the give-and-take skills that make up so much of adult life.

Challenging and arguing with the child, especially if you are not domineering but genuinely interested, will help the child refine her or his thinking abilities and better understand other people's needs. Self-care by parents is essential so that they can continue this challenging and hassling while maintaining warmth and good humour.

Getting ready to leave – 12–18 years

Hard as it may seem (or perhaps you're glad?) this is the age of moving away from family, and moving in again, and away again, practising for the real jump into adult life. Although the child does not yet actually leave, his interests and energies are increasingly outside the family.

Parents also need to have their own interests away from parenting, so that they are not tempted to dominate or be over-involved with their child's world, or to use their child in place of adult company. This is particularly important for single parents.

Some parents feel resentful that this is just a taxi-driving stage – which reflects more on our public transport systems (or lack thereof) and the dangers of our streets at night than anything else. Taxi-ing at least provides a good opportunity to talk.

Three important things are happening:

- The teenager moves forward like the tide – in waves, in and out. One minute he is independent, another wanting to be fed and nursed. One minute he is impressively reasonable, another rebellious and argumentative. Knowing that this will happen makes it easier to handle. Despite the waves, the tide is making progress.
- Sexuality is blossoming. A young person needs to hear that sex is good, that sexuality is welcome and healthy, and that it carries

some decision-making responsibilities. Parents will not act seductively, or respond to seductiveness from the young person.

- The break is going to come. Some young adults move out easily and slowly, but most don't! You can recognise that the young person may need to create and maintain disagreement in order to create the energy to break loose. Don't take this too personally. Like giving birth, releasing young adults is a little painful but well worth the trouble.

THE DOPEY TIME

Around thirteen years of age, most teenagers go through a phase of amazing dopeyness. What is happening is that the puberty hormones are just cranking up, and the sudden growth spurt begins to disorganise their nervous system. Look for the signs — a normally very careful boy knocks over the sugar bowl. A girl goes to school with one sock. They are frequently found about the house standing in a daze, not knowing where they were going or why. In short, a competent twelve-year-old suddenly becomes a hopeless and helpless thirteen.

If you don't know about this stage, you might get very irritated, or think that all your efforts have been wasted! But be patient and kind — they really can't help it. The stage usually lasts only a few months, and all you can do is manage them along, draw lists, help them with their homework. Don't nag too much. It's also a nice gentle phase, when you can be close and affectionate. Soon they will be into the fighting fourteens, so enjoy this stage while it lasts!

KIDS AND TV – THE GREAT DEBATE

Most kids see a lot of TV. In fact, the average child now spends much more time in front of TV than they spend at school! Not just the time spent, but also what is watched is a concern. A child by their mid-teens will have seen tens of thousands of violent incidents, and thousands of deaths, portrayed in cartoon and realistic form – and this is only in children's viewing hours.

The exposure to violence and cheap life values is the most frequent concern about TV watching by kids. The next is what it stops kids from doing – it takes time up which they would normally spend running, jumping, playing, talking, reading and being creative – if they weren't beguiled by the hypnotic flow of the TV screen.

If you're a parent, I ask you to try just one thing – to watch your kids as they watch TV. You may find it a little chilling to see the slightly open-mouthed, blank-eyed stare which kids develop after a time. They are clearly in an 'altered state' – never, in any area of life will you see children so passive and absorbent. By comparison, when reading books, their minds work vigorously as they imagine what the words conjure up. Driving in the car, playing in the yard, going to a circus, they are animated and interactive, 'chewing up' the world with their minds. But in front of the TV they soon drift into that old stare again, the active part of their brain is 'out to lunch'. Have a look for yourself, and judge whether you like what you see.

Young children are particularly affected by what they see on the screen. We once had a four-year-old staying at our house, and he came in for a cuddle before bedtime. We were watching a comedy show, and a sketch came on in which an ET-type creature's hand came out of a cupboard, rejected some chips, and some lollies, but grabbed the child and pulled it in – then burped! It was subtly done, with no real drama – just wry adult humour. I glanced at the child's face though just to check, and noticed his jaw very set. 'Are you okay, Ben?'

'Go away!'

'What are you angry about?'

'That boy got eaten!'

– with which he started to cry, and we spent a good five minutes comforting him and trying to make light of the incident. We were moved by Ben's compassion and a little ashamed that we'd exposed him to unnecessary pain. We wondered if a life of nightmares would ensue! Older kids though, will watch horrific scenes without apparent reaction. Are they desensitised? Is that a bad thing? Of course it is.

Guidelines

If you are a little alarmed and want to do something about what your children watch, here are some suggestions for assessing kids' TV ...

Language – not just swearing – but the quality and richness of verbal skills. Here's a simple test: listen to your child's program for a minute or two without the picture (or go around the corner and listen to the dialogue). Is that the kind of talking you want your child to learn? Aaargh! Urghh! Take that! I'll teach you to ...

Imagination – some kids only know how to play very restricted games – shooting, screaming, hitting. Perhaps this is a symptom that this is all they are watching on TV. It's possible to select kids' TV with a much wider rang of themes. ABC videos, nature videos, they pass the best test of kids' fare – you can stand to watch them yourself! Some movies and programs for kids are simply stunning in imagination, depth and challenge.

Values – this means the hidden message in the film – which has a powerful effect on kids because it is largely unconscious. Common values problems include:

- Bad guys and good guys – some people are villains. They have deep voices and look funny. They are all bad. It's okay to kill them. Some people are all good. They are handsome and bland.
- Conflict is always a result of the bad guys being mean, until the good guys get revenge. It's okay to hurt the bad guys for what they've done. Revenge is sweet. There is no negotiation or middle ground. There are no reasons or sides to the conflict. Action – the more violent the better – is the answer to conflict.
- Sex roles – this is the one that really should have gone away by now. But still in shows from *Superman* to *The Saint*, the girls are cute, beautiful, have high pitched voices, and need rescuing. Boys or men are weapons- and action-oriented, always flying the spaceship, making the decisions, rescuing the girls. And they don't cry – ever!

Advertising – are the shows produced by toy companies to be in effect a half-hour ad for toy figures or accessories? Are the ads all for junk food or overpriced fad toys? Wouldn't it be cheaper if your TV got stuck on the ABC?

News – don't mistake the news for education. It is actually a form of entertainment – and often gives a distorted and unrealistic view of the world. It's not suitable for primary aged children, and we don't think in its present form it does much for adults either. Watching the news can make you paranoid and depressed – and ill-informed about the world we live in.

What about educational TV?

Research has found that *Sesame Street* and similar programs work much better if parents watch alongside their children, from time to time, and sing the songs or comment on the characters, and help their kids 'participate' with the program – in this way avoiding the glazed-eye syndrome once again. The makers of the program deliberately lace the program with subtler humour and ironies to interest adult viewers. They also have rock stars and other celebrities as guests to ensure that parents will turn the show on and occasionally watch it with their kids.

In summary

There are lots of bright spots in kids' TV. *PlaySchool* has remained enormously popular for toddlers because the presenters don't talk down to kids, but TO them, in such a way that kids will often hold conversations with the TV! *Inspector Gadget* must owe part of its popularity to having a smart, capable *girl* child.

Many parents now restrict what their kids watch in quantity and quality. They allocate an hour per day and negotiate which programs. This encourages children to plan, be selective, and savour 'their' program rather than just watching an endless stream.

More and more parents are deciding no have no TV on at all 'till their kids are of school age. Or only a few chosen nature videos as a special treat to give Mum and Did some free time!

HOW TO STOP WHINGEING KIDS

Have you noticed how some adults have really pleasant voices? And that some children also have melodious, clear tones that are a pleasure to listen to? And have you also noticed that there is nothing harder on your ears than a kid who is always whingeing and whining. Talking through their nose? AAAAAWWWWWWW Muhhhhhhhhmmmmmm?

Did you know that the tone of voice we use – as adults or kids – is simply a habit? Not just a habit of voice, but also of attitude to life! Whining comes from the 'helpless' part of us that wants others to fix everything, that is never satisfied, that loves to complain. Whenever we talk with a whinge, we will feel this way too. Whingeing kids, if uninterrupted, will grow into whingeing adults. (Behind every nagging husband or moaning wife is a parent who gave in to a whinger.) But whingeing and whining can be stopped overnight! Here's how ...

First you have to understand how the pattern starts. It's simple enough. A child asks us for something, first of all quietly, then loudly. We say no, or else ignore them. They then move into phase two – they rev up into fullscale whining. It's probably accidental at first – they just discover by chance a tone of voice that we just can't ignore! We will often give in to them, just for some peace and quiet. Before you know it – you have a whingeing kid.

So what do you do?

1. TELL 'EM. Next time they start whingeing at you, make direct eye contact. Then ask them straight out – 'Use a normal voice please'.
2. TEACH 'EM HOW. Find out if they actually know how to speak in a lower sounding voice – firm, but deeper in note. Try them out until they get it right. Demonstrate for them so they can hear what you mean.
3. MAKE IT STICK. Start the campaign. Whenever they whinge at you for anything, say to them 'Use a normal voice'. You are

getting them to realise that whining is not normal – for them, or anyone else. Make sure that they get what they are asking for only by asking more positively.

Of course, if they get to sound like the Queen's New Year speech, don't give in to them if it doesn't suit you – they still have to learn to take no for an answer. 'I liked the way you spoke when you asked me for a biscuit, but I'm sorry you'll have to wait for dinner.'

8

Energy and how to save it

Good news – your children need you healthy and happy.

I once lived for a time in a coastal village of Papua New Guinea. Children there did not live with their own parents but moved about from house to house as they wished! Ten-year-olds could be seen carrying babies or tending cooking fires. By fourteen they were doing adult work with confidence and pride. As the newest and most interesting thing in the village, I had a dozen or so kids sleeping on my veranda. When tropical diarrhoea struck in the small hours of the night, I had to pick my way out through a carpet of small brown bodies!

It occurred to me that this would be an easy place to be a parent since the work and pleasure of parenting was shared by the whole village. In fact, any adult who was present *was* a parent.

In our society, parenting is not shared, and it's not safe for small children to move about the community.

It's easy to feel, then, that you have to become 'Superparent' and somehow meet by yourself all the needs of your kids for entertainment, education, love and affection, food, drink, safety, clothing and cleaning. If you're the one who stays at home with the kids, you feel overdomesticated and housebound and yearn for adult company. If you're the one who goes out making the money, you feel like a workhorse, with too little home and family in your life. It's little wonder that many of us, especially when we have two or more children under five, are almost permanently exhausted, irritable and in borderline health.

When we feel well, and in good company, and healthy and rested, we can give to our children and enjoy doing it. But when we feel tired, sick, lonely and overburdened, there is a point at which kids become a threat, a competitor in the struggle for survival. This condition can easily be dangerous, to you, your marriage and the safety of your kids.

Overstretched parents eventually reach a point at which they can parent no longer. It is vital that you learn to take care of yourself: only then can you parent well. Your kids need you happy and healthy. This brief chapter will tell you how to be and stay that way.

We all need 'fuel'

I often talk with parents who don't understand why they aren't coping. They expect superhuman performance without realising that we human beings need 'fuel'. We don't just run on food: we need 'energy' in the form of love, recognition, touch and talking with others.

Every person you talk to or meet either takes energy away from you or gives you energy. That's why we speak of some people as being 'draining'. It's also the reason we dread certain people ringing us up, or drive for an hour just to see a special friend who makes us feel good.

Kids can give energy back to us, but for the most part it is right and proper that *we recharge them*. However, when we are their only source of refuelling and we dry up on them, something is bound to happen.

Think for a moment. Where is your energy tank right now, as you are reading this book?

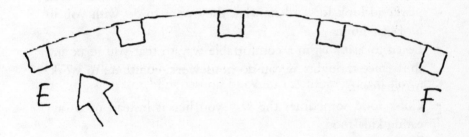

Is this where you usually keep it? Are you always 'running on empty'?

We often treat our bodies as we treat our cars: ten dollars' worth at a time, bald tyres and long overdue for a tune-up!

You might like to look at the people in your life and consider how they help or hinder your fuel reserves. Sometimes people realise that their 'friends' are simply 'stealing' energy and giving nothing back. Time to find some new friends! People who were once good for us (including parents!) may now be a source of only negative feelings. You can, if you wish, change the way you interact with people so that you move to positive exchanges instead.

'Hello, dear, I've had a dreadful week!'

'I've had a good one. Let me tell you about it.'

'God, there were so many problems at the office today.'

'Well, I could listen while you tell me about them. Or would you prefer to plan our next holiday?'

It's a neat strategy and, carried out with good humour, benefits both parties.

With a group of twenty young parents, I once spent a couple of hours listing the ways that parents can 'refuel their tanks'. We came up with quite a few good ideas.

- Get a babysitter.
- Learn to be boring to your children so they leave you in peace for a while.
- Spend 10 minutes with your partner when he or she comes home from work: exchange *good news* or just be together. (If the kids can sit quietly, they can be there; if not, send them into another room.)
- Spend half an hour of *full-attention* time with children each day, instead of hours of begrudged half-attention. Let children plan and look forward to what they want to do with you in *their* half-hour.
- Learn to *switch off* in a comfortable way, so that you relax and think nice thoughts as you do housework, commute to work, or whatever.
- Cook food sometimes the way you like it instead of always eating kids' food.
- Play *your* music.
- Spend plenty of time with other parents.
- Be clear about what you are asking of your partner: affection, sex or just company. Try to meet and understand each other's needs as they arise. If you usually just talk when you're tense, try massage. If you usually just touch, try talking.
- On a regular basis, do one activity that is not concerned with being a parent but is an *adult-satisfying activity*, just for you.
- Have a good escapist book to unwind with at bedtime or mid-afternoon.

- Use all the kinds of support and help around: neighbourhood houses, child health centres, fitness clubs (especially the friendly, non-commercial kind), sports, playgroups and creches, parent effectiveness classes.
- Use a creche or babysitting cooperative for '*self-time*', instead of only for rushing around the shops or to a job.
- Learn that 'Messy Is Beautiful' and give up 'tidy house' ideals for a few years. (You can always leave a vacuum cleaner by the door and say to visitors, 'Gee, I was just about to start cleaning up!')
- Have kids' areas of the house, where valuable things are not around and surfaces and furniture are easy to clean. This saves the wasted energy of a thousand 'don'ts' a day.
- Have tidy and beautiful areas of the house (even if it's only your bedroom) where kids aren't allowed to go – so that you have somewhere nice to be.
- Talk, solve problems, figure out plans in the lounge room, sitting down, face to face, with the kids out of the way. Don't make bed the worrying place. Bed is for better purposes than that.

When some newborn babies 'meet' their mothers, they do not bond well, and changing and feeding are a struggle in which baby and mother are tense and unhappy. One hospital introduced a program for rebonding which is beautiful in its simplicity, and symbolic of the whole parenting process. The staff realised that mother and baby were caught in a vicious circle. They solved this by sitting the mother on a bean bag and the father behind on a chair. The father gently massaged the mother's shoulders and back, enabling her to relax. The mother held and stroked the infant, perhaps feeding it, too. If the mother was a single parent, then a male member of staff would massage the mother instead; and if the father felt tense or awkward, then a physiotherapist might even stand behind him and massage his shoulders.

The unique nature of touch, giving both energy and reassurance, enables humans to soften and move out of tense patterns. It is so often forgotten ... but it beats tranquillisers every time!

But I don't have time for me!

The parents who get most stressed are those who set very high standards and put their own needs far down the list. 'But doctor, I don't understand it. I had just finished redecorating the spare room and baking the three-tiered cake for Tyson's party when this awful headache started. Could you give me something for it because I have to hurry back and finish making Darlene's disco dress?'

In fact, there are three simple responsibilities you have as a parent. Here they are, in order of importance:

- take care of yourself;
- take care of your partnership;
- take care of your kids.

People used to think that, to be a parent, you had to make huge sacrifices and become a doormat. Small wonder that so many people today are opting to have no kids at all. Those same people who saw parenting as a self-denying task can be heard in middle and older life saying things like, 'After all I did for you' and 'We gave you the best years of our life', trying to recapture with guilt the debt they feel is owed to them. The fact is that parenting is something you do for yourself.

It follows, then, that caring for you, your partnership and your kids actually go hand in hand. Looking after yourself makes you happier and more giving – you're giving out of choice, and from a position of fulfilment.

Looking after your partnership reminds you you're a valued and attractive adult, not just a child minder or a breadwinner in the other person's eyes. You have a sense of stability that enables you to relax, but you have enough growth and change taking place to enable you to remain interested in and excited by your partner.

Looking after your kids flows naturally from the above: if you feel that you have chosen parenting as one of your goals, if you are self-caring and have a partnership and friendships that sustain you and remind you of your worth, then giving to children will come easily. Your tank will often be full and your children won't need to start panic buying! End of sermon.

SAVING ENERGY WITH THE 'SOFT NO'

Jerrem is two-and-a-half, and a handful. He seems to have learned infant-assertiveness, and makes demands over and over until something happens – whether it's to have ice-cream for breakfast, to interrupt Mum on the phone, or to get that shiny toy at the supermarket checkout.

His mother, Allie, is luckily discovering how to deal with all of this. Firstly, she knows that this is a normal developmental stage for children of Jerrem's age, and that it won't last forever. Secondly, she has just mastered the 'soft-no' technique, and has become invincible!

She sees other mothers struggle with their two-year-olds, and sees them caught up in rising tension:

I wannit! No
I WANNIT! NO!
I WANNIT I WANNIT I WANNIT
NO YOU CAN'T HAVE IT!

The mothers become angry and tense and upset with themselves, assuming that they must match their infants' red-faced loudness in order to win.

Allie, however, does it differently. She simply says no, quite softly (knowing that children have excellent hearing). If Jerrem persists, she says it again, equally softly, at the same time relaxing her shoulders and softening her whole body (a trick which took a few hours to master). If Jerrem shouts, especially in a public place, she imagines herself carrying him bodily to the car, but at the same time softens and smiles inwardly. She controls her own feelings, rather than letting little Jerrem control them. The temptation to yell at him occasionally returns, but imagining the way he would enjoy this victory, soon removes the temptation.

Allie is puzzled that just as she mastered the 'soft-no' skill, Jerrem seems to have stopped his hassling.

FOOD AND KIDS' BEHAVIOUR

Would you change your kids' diet, if you knew it would make them do really well at school, be calm and happy in themselves, and twice as pleasant to be around? Of course you would. Did you know that poor food intake is thought to be a major factor in juvenile crime? And did you know that the same changes to diet can help *you* to feel better, have more energy, and perhaps avoid being overweight without eating any less?

Sometimes it's important to go back to the basics – and there's nothing more basic than food. What we feed to our children, and when, has a profound effect.

Here are some simple guidelines on the psychological effects of food:

1. CHOOSE FOOD THAT GIVES STEADY ENERGY. Food serves two purposes. It provides nutrients for growing and for repairing our bodies; and it also gives us energy for physical and mental activity. Most people these days provide their kids with a range of foods to give a *nourishing* diet. But it's also important to give the right kind of energising food – complex carbohydrates, and protein foods, which give a steady, day-long energy release. This kind of diet will prevent fatigue, promote a steady, focused state of mind, and help children to feel settled and easy. In particular, children need to eat complex carbohydrates (wholegrain food), high protein food, and perhaps some fresh food such as fruit, for *breakfast* each day.

2. EAT IT BEFORE YOU NEED IT. That's right – breakfast! Breakfast is the meal which will provide energy through the day. Eating substantial foods in the afternoon or evening may nourish you and your kids, but the energy input will be wasted. Eating your main food intake just before you become active will also avoid obesity – food goes straight into the bloodstream where it's needed. When children or adults eat a big meal in the evening, then just sit about or sleep, the food is laid down into their fatty reserves. People can eat just as much, but by changing WHEN they eat it, they'll find that this will reduce weight problems.

   We suggest that you experiment. Give your children protein foods such as eggs, egg-flips, meat or fish with their breakfast each day for two weeks. (If they complain they aren't hungry at breakfast time, give them less for dinner the night before!) See for yourself how much more settled and happy they are at home and school.

3. AVOID 'QUICK BURNOUT' FOODS. Sugar, and refined sugary foods have a remarkably unpleasant effect on kids' behaviour. Many children have simply too much energy minutes after eating such rapid release foods. They become edgy, hyperactive, and just plain naughty. Blood tests show that his energy release peaks early, and the child's blood sugar drops below where it started, as the body struggles to cope. Thus children have a mid-morning sag, where they cannot concentrate, and become lazy and unfocused.

4. AVOID CHEMICALS, DYES AND PRESERVATIVES. Additives and dyes in foods have complex and individual effects.

As well as observing what *your* child reacts to, some foods are generally a problem for almost every child. The need to reduce sugar has already been mentioned especially at breakfast and lunchtime. Tartrazine (E102) which is found in yellow-dyed foods can cause violent hours of hyperactivity in children. Phosphates (found in processed foods such as hot dogs, commercial hamburgers, processed cheese, instant soup and toppings) are also strongly implicated.

The simplest and most effective thing you can do is feed your kids good food earlier in the day – so they just won't get as hungry for junk. Likewise, if your child is going to a party where the parents are still living in the 1950s diet-wise (soft drinks, cakes, ice-cream and lollies!), then feed your kids up before they go – and minimise the damage!

Don't get into big power struggles with food. Just limit the choices to more nutritious food, and hunger will do the trick! And have some leeway for fun foods occasionally.

Appendix

How you can help if you're a teacher, a politician, a grandparent, neighbour or friend.

If you're a primary school teacher: How to counteract negative programming in the children you teach

By the time a child gets to kindergarten you will be able to recognise 'negative programming' very clearly.

Here are the main indicators:

- a child who hangs back from other children, looks sad or agitated and does not respond to overtures of friendship from other children;
- a child who joins in but, when presented with a learning task or activity, will not try it and looks fearful or distracted if approached on a one-to-one basis;
- a child who hits' out at other children and reacts inappropriately when spoken to (for example, by laughing when chastised) and does not seem to have positive exchanges with other children.

You may have children in your class who fall into one of these three categories, or you may find children with a combination of the three.

For the sake of simplicity, let's look at them one at a time.

The sad and lonely child

It is most useful to regard this kind of child as having missed out on affection and on being valued and affirmed in the early part of life (0–2 years). He needs positive messages that are not tied to performance but are simply strokes for 'being', such as 'Hello Eric, nice to see you'. A friendly touch or hug with the child, being careful not to make him seem different from the others, also provides reassurance.

Such strategies, spread out over some days and weeks, should result in the child visibly relaxing and loosening up in the class-room and then beginning to initiate contacts with you – showing you work, smiling at you as you scan the room, speaking to you, and so on.

The self-critical child who won't give things a try

This child may have had her needs met in the early part of life but has been subjected to verbal put-downs consistently since she was old enough to listen (which was, of course, very young). The pattern tends to occur a lot where a mother has a second baby and shifts to being verbally critical of the first child.

Many parents, especially when they themselves are having a tough time, will put their children down as a matter of course, almost every time they speak to them. The children from such situations (probably at least one in ten children) will actually say things like 'I'm stupid', 'I can't' or 'I'm a dumb-dumb' if asked why they won't attempt some new task.

The remedy will be obvious to you: give positive affirmations very consistently to these children. Ideally, give positive messages both for performance and for just being. For example, 'You did that really well', 'I like your ideas for paintings', as well as 'It's nice to see you this morning!' or just plain 'Hello'. Don't gush though – make quiet, understated comments which they can tolerate.

You will have to make sure that you avoid using put-downs with the child (who may actually invite them) and that you use assertive statements rather than 'you' statements to control the child.

For example, use 'Go and get your bag now!' instead of 'You're so forgetful, Anna'.

For really lasting impact, though, the child's parents will need some help, too. You will probably find, if they come to the school, that they are tired, overworked and possibly resentful and defensive. Your best approach would be a casual and friendly chat before broaching the problem, rather than a 'Your kid is a problem' full-frontal attack!

You can simply explain that you have noticed their child's self-esteem is low and he or she may be sensitive to put-downs and be in need of more praise.

Parents of kids in this category will be the ones most helped by reading this book. You could lend them a copy!

The child who is aggressive towards other kids and sarcastic to you

I saved this one till last! This child can be best understood as having been fully hooked on a 'negative' culture, being both handled in an aggressive way and shown by example only negative ways of relating. It is very likely that the child's parents fight routinely, in words if not in actions.

Significantly, the child is not *choosing* to interact using aggression – it may be the only way he or she knows *how* to interact.

It is very important to realise that, initially, this kind of child will not often respond to warmth and praise (but it's worth a try).

The teacher must first of all establish a bond through the mode the child can hear – that of firm engagement. This must be done, of course, without using putdowns.

Thus, in the early weeks, a firm but friendly approach and a clear request for behaviour ('Stop doing that now, and come over here to get a book', 'Sit down now and start your drawing') are the necessary reactions from you.

The way to establish a beneficial and significant relationship with an aggressive child is to persist – firmly and without becoming angry or irritated. Eye contact, especially with humour behind the eyes as you reinforce your firmness, will signal that you are powerful enough to contain the child, so that he or she can begin to relax.

Once this relationship has been established, then positive messages can be added for doing positive things. This differs from what the parents may have done – only noticing the child when he or she played up.

These children are often the most responsive to having special roles (such as 'equipment collector') – roles with a genuine responsibility and privilege. As they develop a 'friendship' with you, that is, the skill of exchanging positive messages – they will be able to extend this to other children.

If you're a secondary school teacher

Negatively programmed children are very much in evidence in secondary schools. In fact, the nature of secondary school can easily worsen the programming.

Often, secondary schools are so factory-like – young people feel they are a nobody, doing what they're told and producing things.

Secondary schools often have huge numbers (often over 1000 in a school, although research suggests that 300–400 is the ideal size); no home base (students are never on their own territory and often even change groupings so that they do not stay with the same friends); and impersonal teaching (learning from so many different teachers, who teach so many classes that they would be hard pressed even to know your name, let alone to care about you.

In my research I have found that students have four major problems with secondary school: the work; sarcasm and put-downs from teachers; loneliness; put-downs and aggression from other kids. It is appropriate for us to address here the last three of these problems.

As a child, I attended a bayside high school near Melbourne. It had a combination (which I later realised was not uncommon) of a gentle, but ineffectual, principal and a vice-principal who was a thug.

On one occasion I saw a boy thrown out of the vice-principal's door and land backwards against lockers on the opposite wall, without touching the ground on the way. This vice-principal had personality traits which would lead me, unhesitatingly (now that I am trained in the field), to seek to have him locked up! Hopefully, things have improved since those days.

Another event that coloured my experience of secondary school was the fate of a close friend who far outstripped the other students academically. Gaining high marks in the final year and securing scholarships to university, he was nonetheless dissatisfied with his own exam performance, bought a rifle and took his own life.

Four children suicided at that school while I was a student there and the school swimming hero went to prison after an unsuccessful fight with drug addiction. We also had many wonderful teachers, great excursions, and a lot of camaraderie. But the whole high school experience had a lot of scope for improvement.

Sarcasm and put-downs from teaching staff

This is a symptom of unhappiness and frustration in the teacher. Few non-teachers have any idea of the stress and difficulty of teaching in secondary schools in the nineties. Teachers come a close second to psychiatrists in the rate of work-caused physical and mental breakdowns.

A large, faceless school isn't any happier for the teacher than for the kids. Secondary schools, fuelled by the breakdown of families and the rise of epidemic unemployment and its hardships, are often physically menacing, emotionally harrowing places unless very concerted and innovative efforts are being made to humanise the school environment.

Sarcasm and aggressive attacks on children are used for two reasons. One is that they simply relieve the teacher's inner pressures: if the teacher was a happier person they would not take place. The second is that control of kids is a constant preoccupation and sarcasm works in getting kids to behave, at least in the short term.

One last plea. We all lose our temper and sound off from time to time. Kids can handle this. It's constant carping that hurts. If you don't basically like and enjoy kids, please don't be a teacher.

Isolation is also epidemic in secondary schools. Watch the school ground or corridor closely during a break. Some students will be visibly alone, others will be attached to cliques and groupings of students, but only loosely so, tagging along but rarely interacting with the others.

Boys will be more tolerant of appendages to their groups: girls tend to include or exclude more decisively. For this reason, you will also see pairs or trios of girls who stay together simply out of mutual loneliness, sometimes barely even talking.

Loneliness

In the classroom you will notice that some children lack even the most basic conversational skills. They will only be able to manage a mumbled word or two if spoken to and would never initiate a conversation unaided. Only recently are some English and speech and drama teachers beginning to tackle these vital skills.

Lonely kids tend to go unnoticed; their more noisy and aggressive counterparts are actually better off since they at least get some of the attention they are seeking. It may take a second look at the classes you teach to spot the loners and wordless ones; they will certainly be there.

If you are willing to 'prioritise' the one or two lonely children in each class, deliberately making contact with them and showing an interest in their work, without drawing down on them the spotlight of class attention, then even this small amount of attention will go a long way to help them gain confidence.

Any efforts to humanise the school experience – such as home rooms and home groups, excursions, camps, peer support schemes and teaching in the areas of social skills, relationships and self-esteem – will be of immense benefit. Secondary school is for many children the last chance to climb out of a negative program for life. Do what you can!

Peer aggression, in action and words

Bullying is not caused by 'bad kids'. The problem is, in fact, always a symptom of the adult system in which the children live. An oppressive overall system, at home or school, leads to the 'victims' taking it out on each other.

From time immemorial, when the barons were tough on the knights, the knights took it out on the peasants, and the peasants beat up their wives and kids. If this dynamic is not understood, school authorities try to stop the persecution with more persecution and the result is even greater tension and violence in the system.

Where teachers are given proper facilities and support in their jobs, and children are treated with firmness but allowed to keep their self-respect, then bullying of kids by kids rapidly dies away. Although material conditions in a school are important, they in no way compare with *how people treat each other*, from the top down.

School is not usually the source of children's more serious problems. Nonetheless, it does have a way of compounding the misery!

In a revealing study carried out for the Council of Adult Education in Melbourne, it was found that illiterate adults had almost universally suffered problems of adjustment before they even entered school. The school, however, failed to remedy the fearfulness and low self-esteem of these children, which became a handicap in their learning to read and write. (One in ten Australian adults have significant literacy problems.)

The failure of schools to help problem children is rarely the fault of the classroom teacher. The fault lies in the whole method of 'factory schooling': we attempt to teach children in herds of 30 to 40 at a time, and wonder that so many do not learn well. We are the only culture in history that has taken such an approach to educating our young; thousands of years ago Aborigines were teaching young people on a one-to-one basis and had few failures or dropouts.

In summary

No teacher, however dedicated, can be both the emotional support and learning stimulus that 30 children need in order to learn well. Soon the day will come when we reassess education and learn to flood our schools with skilled adults, volunteer and paid, trained and training, so that each child gets his or her due. Until then, education will be an uphill battle, with many casualties.

Since you are a caring teacher (or you would not be reading this) and since you want to do as much as you can now, let me conclude by urging you to:

- eliminate put-downs from your classroom and use assertive methods of control;
- when faced with problem children, who may already be taking much of your time and nervous energy, consider using the methods outlined in this chapter;
- be sure to meet your *own* needs for positive strokes and affirmation. You are an endangered species and Australian children need you healthy and alive!

If you're a politician or community activist!

A family is not an island. Healthy families can only exist in a society that supports their needs. Society can be seen as a kind of gigantic social club, to which we all pay membership fees, attend a lot of working bees, and in return receive various benefits.

The social club is far from perfect. Not only is it rather disorganised, but members with vested interests different from our own work constantly change its direction in their favour. We thus have to work hard to make sure that we and others get our part of the bargain, while at the same time being cooperative enough so that the club does not collapse.

Parents in particular find that they need to keep dealing with the world to get a fair deal for their children. Thus, as well as directing energies 'inwards' to improve family life by playing with and educating children, parents may find themselves focusing 'outwards' to society, being on school committees, neighbourhood organisations, right through to a strong political commitment to environmental or other causes.

Naturally people can overbalance in either direction. On one extreme we find the uninvolved family that does not venture into community life, and can thus be herded like sheep into an increasingly totalitarian state. In contrast we find parents who are so politically involved (or career involved, or cause-involved) that they have no family life and so become neurotic and burned out, while neglecting their own marriage and kids.

This book has been an 'inwards' book, dealing with life within the family unit – a worthwhile focus but one needing balance. This brief section looks at how our new understanding of family life affects the wider picture.

The diagram on the following page shows what is sometimes called the 'social contract' – what we receive for our membership in society. The picture looks very 'one-way', but in reality this is not the case. The family gives its labour, taxes, and in many other ways contributes to society. In fact the family multiplied by millions IS society. The family, however, often finds that it is in some way being shortchanged – perhaps health care is poor quality or too expensive, there are no social facilities, or jobs do not exist for the family's teenagers. This requires the family to fight for what it needs.

In dozens of parent workshops I have talked about 'parents' rights', and found that parents are unsatisfied with services, such as schools, doctors, local government, and so on. Allowing for the natural tendency of humans to enjoy a good grumble, it's clear that many people feel powerless and shortchanged by the society around them, and especially by 'the authorities'. The concepts of assertiveness apply here too, and we now teach parents through role-play and strategy-rehearsal to deal with vague doctors, rude public servants, arrogant teachers, and so on, and to get their rights in consumer dealings too.

Assertiveness in the wider arena must include organised action, since single voices only have limited power. More and more in the nineties, people are joining interest groups and movements. No longer do they opt for trivial time-filling groups (the tennis-court-improvement-cake-bake-auxiliary) nor do they favour larger faceless groups such as traditional political parties, but more mid-range movements such as environmental action groups, school involvement groups, and so on.

Politicians should welcome this tendency, since it is the road to real participatory democracy, as well as being a lowcost solution to community development. A caring, close neighbourhood does far more to prevent child abuse (through its removal of loneliness and boredom) than any number of doctors and social workers. Self-help groups such as GROW (for mental health), Parents Anonymous (for child protection), Alcoholics Anonymous, Childbirth Education Association, School Involvement, Parents Without Partners, Vietnam Veterans, are proliferating, and doing a remarkable job.

Friendship
Social facilities
Information

Housing–Food–Water–
Gas–Fuel–Electricity–
Telephone

Policing–
National Defence

Transportation–
Sewage–Health Care

Recreation–
Entertainment–
Education

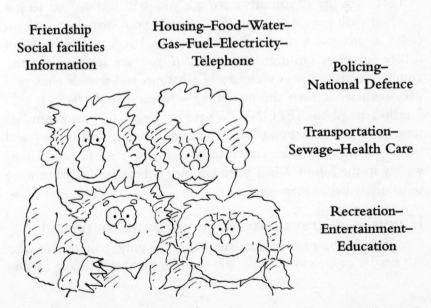

There is no doubt that families need material security first. Below a certain income level, no one can raise happy children. However, above a basic level the need changes. What people benefit from most once they are housed and fed adequately is a chance to be connected with others and involved in purposeful activity which has been freely chosen. One often hears the complaint that parents 'don't want to get involved'. Usually this complaint comes from someone who conducts boring and alienating parent-teacher nights or preachy lectures on how to bring up children! Contrast this with the immense success of parties for looking at and buying plastic bowls and lacy underwear! Clearly people love to involve themselves in friendly, participatory gatherings, and will risk a surfeit of lunch boxes to do so! It's sad that such trivial gatherings are often the only way to meet the strong needs for belonging and interaction in our vast suburban homelands.

A large-scale statistical study in the US sought to find out why in spite of low income, broken homes, and poor housing, some teenagers remained law-abiding and productive, while others became criminal offenders. The only factor which emerged clearly was that those who coped had access to adult involvement, outside their family, which was supportive and friendly. Most often, though not in all cases, this was through belonging to some club or group led by interested adults. Since incarceration of young offenders costs about $60,000 per person per year, youth work also seems a sound investment.

Let's sum up. If you are a parent, you will often need to get involved with groups and situations outside your own four walls, in order to advance your family's interests, and secure some kind of future for your children to live in. If you are involved in the community, whether as secretary of a parents-and-friends club, or a parliamentarian, then the one thing you must understand is that families need to BELONG. Whatever helps to bond families together and build strong local communities will save money and trouble a hundredfold, and lead to a happier more self-reliant society in the future. When public money is being spent, prevention is definitely better than cure.

If you're a grandparent, neighbour or friend

Parenting can be a lonely business. Often it is only those people who live nearby or are close family who see the pressure building up and the negative put-down patterns beginning to develop between parent and child. It's difficult in this position, though, to know how to offer help in a way that won't offend. Let me make some suggestions.

Practical help

The most obvious way you can help is babysitting. Many young parents are exhausted from the sheer endlessness of parenting and earning a living. A couple of hours' relief may be life-saving, and yet is something that parents hesitate to ask for, for fear of imposing on you. Here's a hint: offer to babysit 'sometimes' and do so, but occasionally say, 'No, I won't be able to this week'. This lets the parents know that you can say no – and also means you won't be taken for granted! A friend of mine, who is crafty to match her years, offers to babysit for some young parents next door only if they agree to use the time for relaxation. Manipulative but effective.

Material help comes next. Our society seems to be built on a pattern whereby we are poor when we are raising our children, and have an excess of money when our children are grown up. In earlier times people were individually poorer, but could *share* in the family's collective property. The loan of all the equipment needed for raising children (prams, etc) or other forms of material support is much appreciated by today's young family.

Friendship

There is nothing like warm, good-humoured availability, and a willingness to listen, in a neighbour or friend. Parents accumulate tension and worries as they go along and, with a sympathetic listener, these will tend to pour off like water off a duck's back. If you have the time to listen and enquire, and if you don't rush in with remedies or comparisons, you will visibly notice the relaxation spread on the person's face as he or she talks.

Don't preach, teach, judge, compare, criticise, evaluate or generally act like Dorothy Dix. If you feel the patronising glow of 'older and wiser' coming over you, then close your mouth and smile a lot until the feeling passes. Advice can be a blow to the self-esteem of the person receiving it, especially if it wasn't sought in the first place. Even if it's 'good' advice, it will have the unpleasant side-effect of making the person feel small. Take my advice!

What *not* to do

If you are the parent's parent, you will be tempted again and again to slip in some of the parenting you overlooked when they were twelve years old, just at the moment when they are floundering and hoping you hadn't noticed. If you do this often your offspring will have to pretend to be coping whenever you're around – an added burden for them.

Adults need friends, not parents, and they need positive messages.

Supplementary parents

Margaret Mead once said that little kids and grandparents get on so well because they have a common enemy! Kids do need other adults, as friends, parents confidantes, and to give approval and affection at those times when parents are just too overtaxed to respond well. I know of many people who only made it through their childhood because in an otherwise unbearable home life there was one older person nearby who provided a safe harbour. Even the crabbiest grandparent has his value, if only to show that Mum and Dad really are quite nice people by contrast!

When families are woven in with friends and neighbours, and when people of all generations have access to each other, then we won't need psychologists or departments of social welfare. We'll take care of ourselves.

A STORY TO END WITH

A good friend of mine told me this story about an everyday incident at his house, which kind of sums up the whole parenting business. It's about being human and making mistakes and how, as we don't quit, things have a way of working out.

My friend had had a bad day at work. He was tired, it was hot, the house was a mess. It was getting late in the evening.

His oldest boy, a largish thirteen-year-old, was crowding around in the kitchen in that way that teenage boys seem to, kind of taking up all the space at once. Some little argument flared up. The father suddenly found himself yelling, 'Look just get out of here. Go to your room. I'm sick of you!'

The boy stormed off to his room. Within seconds, the father felt ashamed. He had seen the boy's face as he yelled, seen his eyelids flinch at the violence of his father's anger. He realised the boy would have been physically afraid at that moment.

He tried to figure why he had been so angry. It didn't fit the situation. Perhaps it was just the day. Either way, the feeling of shame didn't go away.

After a few minutes, he went up to the boy's bedroom, and said sorry. 'I shouldn't have yelled at you. You were hassling me, but it didn't deserve me shouting or sending you away. I'm sorry and I'd like to ask your forgiveness.'

Ouch! It takes guts to do this, it really hurts even just to write this. The boy was very noncomittal. His feelings were hurt, a few words saying 'sorry' were hard to trust. The father went downstairs and cleaned up the kitchen.

After twenty minutes or so, he went up to go to bed. He was in the bathroom brushing his teeth when the son ambled past on his way to the toilet. The youngster had a twinkle in his eye, and spoke softly, but very clearly, as he walked through – '*How come it's so hard to hate you?*'

You put a lot in with your kids, from the sleepless nights and the frightening trips to the casualty department, through to homework assignments and a million miles of taxi-driving.

The great thing is that everything you put in counts, and with a bit of luck, one day they will realise it. Love adds up to something. Nothing else matters half as much.

References

These are some of the books used as sources or cited in the book.

Axline, Virginia, *Dibs*, Penguin, London, 1980.

Biddulph, Steve and Shaaron, *The Making of Love*, Doubleday, Sydney, 1988.

Embling, John, *Tom a child's life regained*, Pelican, New York, 1980.

Gordon, Thomas, *Parent Effectiveness Training*, Plume, New York, 1970.

Illsey-Clarke, Jean, *Self-Esteem: A Family Affair*, Winston, Oak Grove, MN., 1978.

James and Jongeward, *Born to Win*, Addison Wesley Longman, Reading, Mass. 1971.

Liedloff, Jean, *The Continuum Concept*, Futura, London, 1975.

Schiff, Jacqui, *All Our Children*, Ballantine, New York, 1983.

York, David and Phyliss, *Tough Love*, Bantam, New York, 1983.

Further information (for those who work with children)

My goal in writing this book is to help parents recognise and eliminate what I call 'put-down parenting' – the use of destructive messages as a form of child control. All the chapters following the first are there to provide alternatives to the putdown style, so that parents may relinquish it and not be left at a loss for what to do instead.

Childcare and counselling professionals may recognise many of the concepts used in this book; however for those wishing to trace particular ideas to their source, or to explore the implications for helping families and children, a brief summary of sources for each chapter follows:

1. Seeds in the mind

The significance of childhood 'taping' of parental messages was first recognised by Eric Berne, and is a central part of the treatment system known as Transactional Analysis. Robert and Mary Goulding systematised the negative programming of children into ten basic 'DON'T' messages, and found that it was not passive programming (as Berne had believed), but an 'out-of-awareness' cooperation by the child that allowed the messages to remain in action, often severely impairing adult life chances. Tracing and bringing into awareness this programming forms a powerful treatment technique known as 'Redecision Therapy'.

Children who have been severely deprived and/or disturbed may lack replacement messages even if placed in a caring environment. Jacqui and Aaron Schiff demonstrated success with a system of intensive reprogramming of such children, with highly directive and highly nurturant components, known as 'Reparenting'.

The concept of 'accidental hypnosis' is directly attributable to the work of Milton Erikson, and is described both in his own books and the many books written about him since his death. In particular, Richard Bandler and John Grinder have made clear how this process takes place and also how it can be deliberately used. The ethics of this are currently being debated.

'You-messages' were popularised under that name by Thomas Gordon, in the immensely successful Parent Effectiveness system.

Under the name of 'attributions' they are discussed in almost any Family Therapy text, for instance books by Virginia Satir, Jay Haley, R. D. Laing, etc.

2. What children really want

The early work of Rene Spitz, John Bowlby and others, and writing on the conditions known as hospitalism and marasmus led to the concept of 'positive strokes'. The whole behaviour modification approach builds on this concept – that 'what you stroke is what you get'. Amelia Auckett's book on Baby Massage is a good introduction to affectionate parenting.

3. Curing by listening

Or 'Active Listening', evolved from Carl Rogers' client-centred counselling, as applied to everyday situations. Once again Thomas Gordon takes credit for making this approach available to parents.

4. Kids and emotions

Emotions are best understood as variants of the four biological states – anger, fear, sadness, joy. While these are innate, the expression of them is shaped by familial and cultural factors to an enormous degree. Counselling theory and practice – for instance, ReEvaluation Counselling – is helpful in understanding and freeing up the emotional side of being human. The systematic teaching of expressive and yet socially constructive emotional responses was developed by the Reparenting school of Transactional Analysis. The concept of 'racket' or phoney emotions aimed at controlling others, is an important one. Tantrums, shyness, and sulking or boredom are very common childhood disturbances of emotion which are tolerated too much in our culture, and so often continue into adult behaviour – as violence, depression, and so on. Ken and Elizabeth Mellor first taught us about the false nature of shyness, and how to 'cure' it.

5. The assertive parent

Assertiveness is widely known and taught, but not often applied directly to parenting. This is a pity because if parents were assertive, they would not need to use put-downs. Adequate books and courses on assertiveness deal with the surface skills; the really useful books and courses help parents look at their own negative programming.

The 'Tough Love' movement looks very worthwhile for parents with problem kids, though good liaison with professionals is needed for self-help groups to succeed.

6. Family shape

Margaret Mead, in her irrepressible way, did most to remind us that we no longer live in real families, but in fragments of families. More elaborated ways to look at intrafamily structure are taught by Virginia Satir, Michael White, Brian Cade or any 'structural family therapy' source.

7. Ages and stages

The developmental stages used in this book were based on the work of Pamela Levin. Jean Illsley-Clarke's book (listed in '*References*') which expands Levin's ideas further, is a useful and down-to-earth child development guide by ages and issues.

8. Energy and how to save it

The experience of being 'drained' by some people, and of giving and receiving energy to and from others, is almost universally acknowledged by parents. The work of Ken Mellor and Julie Henderson and other 'bioenergeticists' points to this being more than just a metaphor, and can be lifesaving for those parents for whom exhaustion is a daily hazard. Approaches such as Reiki, massage and relaxation can all be invaluable for parents, and should be made more available.

Other books by Steve Biddulph

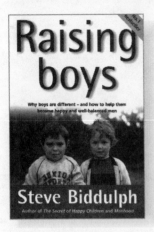

Everyone who has boys today is concerned for them. Everywhere we look, boys are having trouble with their lives. Parents want to understand better what makes boys tick, and how to help them be happy, loving and capable.

In *Raising Boys*, Steve Biddulph looks at the most important issues in boys' developments from birth to manhood – and discusses the warm, strong parenting and guidance that boys need. He brings his humour, honesty and practical knowledge of families to the vital task of raising our sons.

Since its release in 1994, *Manhood* has had a profound emotional impact on thousands of men and women. Copies have been passed from hand to hand (by friends, partners, workmates and family) with the simple message, 'You must read this!'

Manhood tackles the key areas of a man's life – parenting, love and sexuality, finding meaning in work and making real friends. It opens new pathways to healing the past and forming true partnerships with women, as well as honouring our own inner needs. This revised and expanded edition captures the spirit of change that is giving men new hope for a better future.

The newly revised edition of *More Secrets of Happy Children* tackles the important concerns of parents in the nineties, with inspirational ideas and clues for day-to-day living with children.

Raising Boys and *Manhood* (published by Finch Publishing) and *More Secrets of Happy Children* (published by HarperCollins) are available in bookstores.